ELEMENTS ON THE JOURNEY

Learn different ways
of how to integrate
nature's wisdom into your life.

BY CHRISTELLE CHOPARD

Copyright © 2013, 2015 by Christelle Chopard
All rights reserved, including the right of reproduction in whole or in part in any form.

DHARMI® is registered trademark of Christelle Chopard. All drawings and artwork used in this book, including all cover illustrations are original artworks, and are Copyright © 2011, 2013, 2015 in the United States by Christelle Chopard, and in part, by Julio Ferraresi. Permission to publish the drawings and artwork has been received by Julio Ferraresi.

Library of Congress Cataloging-in-Publication data.

Published by Christelle Chopard, DHARMI® Institute for
Holistic Self-Development, Miami, Florida.

ISBN-13: 978-1517586171

ISBN-10: 1517586178

This book reflects the views and personal experience of the author. This book is not intended as a guide to independent self-healing or therapy.
If you have any specific questions, or insights you like to share, contact the author at: info@dharmi.com.

This book is dedicated...

> *to you*
>
> *to the wise teachers who crossed my path*
>
> *to life-learning experiences*

OVERVIEW

Chapter One 17
        Key Elements for Manifestation and Liberation
        The Cycle through the Elements
        What are the key aspects of The Cycle through the Elements?

Chapter Two 35
        The Elements on the Journey
        The Element of Earth—Form
        The Element of Water—Flow
        The Element of Fire—Shine
        The Element of Air—Clarity
        The Element of Ether—Essence
        The Four Pillars

Chapter Three 47
        Elements for Holistic Self-Development
        Key Elements for a Healthy Lifestyle: Living With Well-Bing—Earth Element
        Emotional Intelligence and Relationships: Considering the Flow of Emotions - Water Element
        How Far Should We Go in a Relationship?
        Self-Esteem and Leadership
        Key Elements for Healthy Self-Esteem
        Making Decisions Using the Five Elements
        Letting Go of Attachments
        Mindfulness & Stress Management
        Key Elements for Stress Awareness & Management
        Life's Transition: Life is a Constant Evolution—Ether Element
        Loss Ushered in a New Chapter
        Separation and Divorce Lead to a New Career
        Losing Your Job—Gaining Your Integrity
        Creating a Support System
        Honoring Our Feminine Energy

Chapter Four 109
        Cycle for Creation & Manifestation
        Space and Time Management
        In a Business Setting, the Five Elements are Also Important
        Key Elements from Inspiration to Manifestation
        Part of My Story
        Completion of Cycles and Liberation
        Completion of a Cycle in a Relationship or Separation
        Paths Sometimes Diverge
        Completion of a Cycle at Work

Chapter Five 149
        Key Elements for Communication
        Presence-Awareness
        Reflection-Mindfulness
        Expression and Leadership
        Emotional Intelligence and Influence
        Manifestation, Sense of Space and Ownership (Earth)
        Inspiration-Liberation

Chapter Six 193
        The Elements for Balance and Healing
        Integrating the Elements for Balance & Healing
        Phases in Self-Development
        Main Stages in Life
        Foot Analysis, based on the Grinberg Method™
        The Elements and Holistic Foot Analysis
        Did You Know that Your Footprints Reveal Your Life's Path?
        Holistic Foot Analysis and the Elements
        Exploring the Flow Through the Elements
        The Elements for Dance and Self-Expression
        The Five Elements in Meditation
        Integration
        Integrating the Elements in Healing Through Touch
        Elements in Mandala Design for Healing and Balance

Conclusion 247
Glossary 249
Appendix: Other Pathways on the Map 251

Author Biography

The fundamental steps set forth in this book have been written based on my ideas, research and inspiration. I am Christelle Chopard, founder of the DHARMI® Institute. Through my studies as well as my personal and professional experiences, I found a clear Map, which led to a higher level of consciousness and, when I shared the MAP, has helped many people achieve balance, a higher vibration and harmony in their lives.

I received clarity through my meditations and DHARMI practice, as well as through my studies and experiences with enlightened beings on five continents. It has been a quest that has taken me on a journey through external and internal worlds.

I noticed that from this foundation and by making use of these principles in life, the alignment in our evolution is supported and abundant. The three pathways (which are the Cycle of Evolution, The Vortex of Energy Meditation, and the Cycle through the Elements) form a trio that opens access to our true intention, aligns our vibrations, and unveils our life's purpose, step-by-step.

THREE PATHWAYS IN THE DHARMI® MAP

Cycle of Evolution

Cycle of Energy

Vortex of Energy

I discovered this Map while traveling through more than 40 countries, experiencing and studying different traditions, cultures, spiritual and holistic approaches. I then followed the inner guidance, spurred on through signs around me and clarified through profound meditation. I have been inspired by a clear vision to follow this route, since I began receiving messages and signs at a young age, eventually leading to the revelation of my mission—that of helping lead others to fulfill their own paths thorough the DHARMI Map.

My discipline, dedication, compassion, and unbridled sense of adventure, combined with a true wish to help add to the well-being, peace and happiness in my fellows, led me onwards down a long path that became a quest and led to the discovery of the Map.

I realized the time had come to share my discovery and reveal the Map's teachings to the wider world. Here I share a part of the journey that led me to such revelation:

My inspiration came from life's creation and nature's wisdom; my personal experiences traveling the world as a healer, holistic consultant and mentor; and my studies of the Grinberg Method™ of personal development, as well as the Vipassana Meditation, and lessons in shamanism and studies in tantric energy practices.

My training also included certification as a handwriting expert with the Handwriting Analysis University in California and with the institute of Graphology and Graphotherapy in Spain. I am well-versed in holistic therapies and consulting, craniosacral therapy, Qigong, movement-dance therapies, meditation and yoga. I was an instructor, producer and South American coordinator and participated in leadership programs with Condor Blanco, an organization that teaches courses in professional and personal development to help people align their actions and their dreams.

From an early age I was inspired to follow my own dreams. Bidding my home goodbye at age 18, I worked to support myself to be able to study my passions—healing, personal and spiritual development. I was inspired to learn from my life's experiences, to awaken mindfulness in the community and to manifest my purpose step-by-step on the journey. At the age of 22, I started my own company, concentrating on holistic therapies and consulting. Since then, I have taught and traveled worldwide, adding to my knowledge and experience.

In 2011 all the pieces came together. I discovered the Map that would support a harmonious flow, balance and development into my life and the lives of so many others.

Since then, I have written ten manuals and have shared the steps I've followed with searchers in communities in the Americas, Europe and Australia. In 2014, I opened the physical location of the DHARMI Institute in Miami, Florida. This book makes the third books and one journal published to help present the three pathways found in the Map: The Cycle of Evolution, La Voie de la resonance - The Vortex of Energy Meditation, The Cycle through the Elements and Key Elements For Holistic Development, a journal/diary in which to write your insights and follow your journey with the guidance of the Map.

I combined the studies of diverse sciences that explain the relationship between thoughts and physical manifestation, as well as the emotional memory and our behaviors. I explored ancestral traditions throughout Europe, Asia, Australia, the Americas and Africa. Through undertaking vision quests, as shamans have been doing since the dawn of time, the portal to spiritual balance and physical health became ever clearer.

The Map is a holistic GPS that supports you as you navigate through the many ways, the many paths, and the many perspectives, speaking to your uniqueness, yet beckoning you to oneness with your community and environment.

The DHARMI philosophy promotes new levels of awareness to support real shifts in your life and perspective. The Map will honor the fact that you are a unique individual that there is no one like you, yet you are one with all. It also attests to the fact that communication is one of the most effective tools to use on the holistic path to evolution.

Such conscious communication segues into the steps of The Cycle through the Elements.

This cycle considers the Five Fundamental Elements of Air, Fire, Water, Earth, and Ether to help you reach a state of love, balance, abundance and success.

The process will help support your personal evolution and help inculcate healthy values, true integrity and compassion. My intention is to support you in responding to your needs, ordering your priorities, and realizing your dreams, while supporting the well-being, peace and happiness in the community.

- DHARMA MAP -

INTRODUCTION

No man is an island. We are all influenced by each other, by our environment and community, but we are equally influenced by how we perceive ourselves, our standing in our community and our place in the world-at-large. How we see ourselves, our perspective, dictates our approach toward everything in our life. It affects our thoughts, actions, feelings, relationships and also our health.

This book is for people who are willing to take leadership in their lives, for those of you who choose to create an inspiring perspective, based on healthy values and positive intentions.

Sometimes, for not knowing another way, we can become victims, letting ourselves drift away from our values, our goals and our intentions. We can even let die those divine sparks that come from the inspiration of others. But there are tools to support you to take leadership and bring mindfulness through your actions, decisions, and direction in your life.

We can recognize that core beliefs influence our thoughts, decisions, and perspective. Statements like "I can't", "I'm not good enough", "I haven't enough strength", "I'm not that smart", "I'm too independent", "Good things never happen to me" or "I'm too strong" often make themselves manifest in our lives.

We can learn to claim our own power, to take ownership of our own lives and, with that ownership, the responsibility for creating the type of life that nurture our healthy values, and is aligned with our intentions.

We are here in this life to create as an artisan creates—works of art unique unto ourselves. We create our lives and, as we do so, we help others around us create their lives. Each of us is a singular soul, unlike anyone who came before or will come after us. We generate unique thoughts and feelings, based on our own experiences and perspective. These thoughts and feelings generate energies and vibrations that we can learn to use to manifest in our lives. If those vibrations come from thought and feelings of love and acceptance, we can reflect that love into our relationships and our everyday actions.

When we engage in a process of holistic self or professional development, we can learn to open ourselves to such vibrational energy. By learning to harness our own unique energy, we can balance the Five Elements (Earth, Water, Fire, Air, and Ether) to reflect, express and manifest a positive intention.

When we develop more awareness of the Five Elements, we can channel, direct and manifest our intention with confidence, compassion, and clarity.

Many people think that they are afraid of their shadow or of failure. Yet, I have noticed that most of the people are afraid of success. It takes courage and requires a certain level of surrender, to tune in, to allow our own gifts to shine and vision to manifest. We can learn to access our internal force, to manage it with a clear direction on where and how to direct it. This book inspires you to not back down from facing the experience, feeling your power and potential, and to make use of it for a higher purpose. I invite you to explore how nature's wisdom and fundamental Elements can support you to shine, surrender, and manifest your health (Earth), relationships (Water), self-esteem (Fire), state of mind (Air) and overall sense of well-being and purpose (Ether).

You can nurture a state of love, compassion, generosity, and forgiveness in yourself and add such vibrations to the world. You will not find such things outside yourself, until you find such things within. It is a state of being that you can experience fully when you open yourself to that vibration. By consciously using your creative energy to develop your gifts and potentials, you will change your experience of the world. By changing your perspective, the world itself will change.

I hope this book will inspire you to move through life's transitions with integrity, acceptance, and abundance.

- DHARMA MAP -

CHAPTER ONE
Key Elements for Manifestation and Liberation

There are Five Elements that function in your life and they affect five corresponding areas of your existence—your health, relationships, self-esteem, state of mind, and overall sense of well-being. As a whole, they steer you towards developing clear values, living with integrity and clear intention. Also, they support you in experiencing harmony in all things. Aided by healthy, holistic lifestyles choices, emotional sobriety, the use of proper introspection and meditation and correct choices about your professional development, your life can unfold with grace and balance. These Five Elements that will be discussed and how we can integrate them into different aspects of our lives are Ether, Air, Fire, Water and Earth.

Nature is the most beautiful and functional creation you can turn to as a model.

No matter how worldly or sophisticated or even cynical we become, the truth is we are one with the other inhabitants of this planet—the animals, plants and fellow humans—who share this fragile blue globe. We are as affected by weather, the passing of the seasons, damage to our environment and the passage of time as any of our fellow creatures.

These external aspects make as much of an impact on us and how we view the world as our age, our emotions, our perspective or our circumstances. The earth spins. Mother Nature gives birth and presides over deaths. Time truly does march on and the natural world gracefully bows to such changes. Not so man. People come into the world screaming. That first scream is symbol of liberation. Yet many of us spend the years after that striving and fighting and clawing our way to worldly success, trying to fulfill expectations and creating attachments, until we face the inevitable loss of all that we have spent a lifetime collecting. How much more serene would we be if we could learn balance, how to live our lives gracefully, while manifesting our inspirations and visions and honoring healthy values and relationships? We can grow, manifest, and have a harmonious, abundant life with family, home and society, while respecting our intention, time and space with a balanced lifestyle. When we allow beauty, acceptance, and love into the process of creation, we then can surrender, with no argument when our time on earth passes by. To everything there is a season...even for our lives.

In the balanced life that I am suggesting you embark upon, there are many paths, side roads, forms of study and interpretations of the knowledge gained. I can only share my perspective with you here. I invite you explore, to open yourself to experiences, to add new possibilities into your life. The path I introduce you to here can be a perfect complement to other philosophies, practices or methodologies. Follow your own path and feel free to share what you discover with me.

The Five Elements already introduced—Ether, Air, Fire, Water and Earth—are derived from nature, and used in a holistic approach to lifestyle, well-being and development. They can be used as tools to manifest and create our reality. We can apply their wisdom in our lives every day, and make it a discipline to do so. We need ongoing training and to pay strict attention to use these Elements to manifest a vision or an intention so that they may serve our purpose in this lifetime. Treat them with care and respect, for they can help heal you, get you closer to your heart center, and help you grow with healthy values.

Familiarizing yourself with and making use of each Element is important to help you find balance, live with harmony and integrity and to make manifest those things you want to bring forth in your life. Yet each person has a dominant Element that, though it interacts and complements the others, has a stronger influence on his or her life. By learning with Elements, we can clarify some thinking and make better use of our strengths, emotional intelligence, and resources. We can strengthen our character assets, lessen our defects and make the best use of our potential.

Often a weakness around one of the Elements may be due to a lack of attention paid to it and its effect in our lives. It can also be caused by traumas along your path or by your heritage, karma, in your DNA or your spiritual evolution.

Perhaps you have fallen into the trap of keeping your focus on someone else's expectations—wishing you could be like them (or hoping you could change them), so that you have no attention left to focus on your own intention in the relationship. Maybe you were brought up to think that paying attention to your reactions, sensations, feelings and own beliefs was selfish and therefore bad. Perhaps you never felt worthy of such careful, mindful attention. Paying attention to one's self is just like placing an airplane's oxygen mask over your own face first before turning to help a child or seatmate. If you don't care for your own intention, projections, behaviors and forms of expression, there is no connection with others around you. And you are worthy of attention. We all are. Disregarding our fundamental needs, or refusing to look inward to see what they are in the first place, will lead us to rely too much on one or two Elements as opposed to all five. In this case, you are thrown out of alignment to a degree that can cause stress and more disconnection for you and your environment in the long run. Yet we also have to take in consideration that we all have specific gifts or one or more stronger Elements than the others, which gives us the chance to complement our gifts with other people's whom we meet on our journey.

You must look at yourself; striving for clarity of vision about who you truly are and what you want and need is important to consider before you can begin to restore balance in your life. Without such mindfulness, you are forfeiting the personal responsibility that can support you in creating a clear communication, loving relationships, healthy thinking and a balanced lifestyle.

You will have different priorities, potentials and perspectives from other people, but, deep inside, most of us are looking for peace, compassion, happiness, freedom and abundance.

Freedom can be interpreted in many ways. When I speak about freedom, I am referring to a state of being that develops when we respect our values, honor our intention and fulfill our life's purpose. In other words, freedom is living our dharma—accepting our destiny, and leading our way through life with bliss, love and compassion—towards ourselves and others.

Freedom is a powerful experience that reflects a willingness to own and accept the responsibility of being you—the you that shines with full potential, in connection to your heart, core values and intentions. Freedom is a powerful place to be. It requires both grace and respect.

I have met people who can't live without conditions that can't be met, unfulfilled expectations and overly dependent attachments. Such people are moving through their lives with fear, stress and insecurity.

I have met other people who try to detach from everything. By protecting themselves from emotional attachment to others, they deny the fundamental principle of the universe—that of love. They form warped values, close their hearts and deny their life's purpose.

Neither of these extremes is a satisfying way to live. Though, we may have to pass through some of those cycles to learn and to redefine our direction. Sometimes we have to get lost to find our way.

Freedom charts the middle course, allowing us to be fully who we are, completely alive, enjoying healthy relationships with ourselves and our fellow man, at peace with our surroundings and adding our own welcome contribution to the cauldron of life.

Each person has his or her own right path to this freedom, his or her own steps to follow in the dance and to tread the floor lightly, with as much compassion and intention as you can summon up, secure in the knowledge that such a road will lead to a place of bliss and balance.

Freedom requires devoted discipline, constant evolution, clear purpose, and focused intention. You have the possibility to renounce your limitations, awaken your creativity and allow a nurturing flow of abundance into your life.

Resistance or weakness will fall by the wayside and obstacles will be swept away as you access your true potential, notice new possibilities and open your heart to abundance, compassion, and clarity.

Some people have an abundance of awe-inspiring inspirations and transformative ideas. These are the artists that paint amazing visions, lift our spirits with their words or transport us with their music. Yet some of them may find it difficult to pay their bills at the end of the month, to find the resources to support the manifestation of their mission. Some of them may have the gift, yet they don't find a direction, therefore they have trouble manifesting their dreams. If that is the case, it is an invitation to reflect and consider what Elements are missing. Also, perhaps the person has this potential and need only find someone else who has the gifts that complement and help them make the best use of their own.

Others suffer from resistance to new inspiration and creative ideas—such as an author stymied by 'writer's block'. They may choose to ignore their creative gifts and spend their time and spiritual capital working very hard in an unrelated field. They may have to focus their time and energy on making money and supporting their needs or the needs of their family. Their true soul purpose is relegated to a hobby or put aside entirely, with the artisan promising herself that "someday" she'll return to her talent, yet putting off the dawn of that someday for years and perhaps never making use of it at all. A spiritual gift squandered can lead to a sense of frustration, stress and even depression. When that happens, it is a sign that it is time to reflect and redefine the direction of their potential. It is not only about 'what' we do, but also about 'how' we do it. The inner potential, intention and talents can be used to perform a job, to take care of family, to nurture others and ourselves. It doesn't have to be repressed in order to be productive and fulfill our worldly responsibilities.

Take a sharp look at yourself right now. *Are you creatively expressing your gifts and using your creative talent in your life?*

If not, you can learn to clarify, heal and unveil your gift and creative potential using the tools provided in this book. Perhaps you can lead your actions from a healthier and more loving place.

Don't act from unrealistic expectations, poor judgment or from a feeling of victimization. Instead, search within your heart, your higher self and set your preference. You can generate any frequency of energy and manifest a life experience that reflects this intention. Don't doubt this nor question it. You are the author of your own experiences—you are writing the story of your life. That story can speak with the voice of the ego or the voice of the heart, honoring your own potential, truth and path. Based on your own interpretation and your own illusion of a world around you, you generate anything that affects you, from the outside in and the inside out. You can perceive people, your environment and daily circumstances, with love and compassion.

Whenever you go outside of yourself with preset expectations, you are actually letting go of your own inner compass, losing touch with your own frequency and your own generated energy. By doing so you deny what you truly feel by directing your power to something or someone outside of yourself. Whether it is a lover or a job or material things, by distancing yourself from your intention and values, you are losing your self and distancing yourself from the lover, job or material things.

The main purpose of the Map and The Cycle through the Elements is to recognize and honor your process of evolution and development. There is no shortcut to evolution. When you follow your heart and the steps on your journey, your purpose and mission unfold step-by-step.

You may not be a Gandhi, a Nelson Mandela, a Rumi, an Einstein, or a Madre Teresa. Yet, you have a mission within the community. You have your role to fulfill. We all do, and we cannot compare ourselves to anyone else. Each of us is different, yet each of us is equally precious and connected.

You will find peace, contentment and fulfillment when you are aligned with your heart and vision. When you integrate the Five Elements mindfully for your balance and expression, you will build confidence as you grow, clarify your path and your values and honor them.

However, we may have experienced stress, unmet expectations and hurtful conditions within our family or disappointments in our community that have affected us and colored our view of life. Perhaps we have become cynical, guarded, resentful or more attached. We are also programmed and influenced by the media, cultural expectations, judgments from others and reactions to our surroundings. There are so many experiences and influences along the road of our beautiful journey. So is it in nature, when a tree falls near a river and influences its course.

We are blessed to live in a time of awakening; a time where time and space can be transcended with new technology and tools. Even the daily bombardment of our senses from the internet, social media and noise can serve to help our evolutionary progress, if used properly. Used improperly, of course, it can provide us with excuses to keep us from focusing on our personal growth and distract us from our responsibilities to our environment and community. Time better spent in reflection and meditation can be squandered staring at a flickering computer screen. Finding a balance will support us to grow and develop healthy relationships. Learning to give space and attention to all fundamental aspects will support our evolution and well-being. It can do the same for the ones who cross our path, whether we meet those people in person or connect with them online.

We live in a world filled with instant gratification that can feed addictive natures and encourage patterns of communication that feed into unhealthy behaviors and thoughts, creating vicious circles. We will never gain fulfillment within any situation until we open our minds and hearts to fully experience it.

In some cities, we can miss the feel of the earth beneath our feet and fingers, the sight of fruit ripening, the taste of its juices dripping down our chin, the satisfaction we feel when the harvest is safely gathered. We can forget about the deliciousness and quality and accept an unhealthy diet based on fast food. Some of us are no more connected to that food than we would be downing a mouthful of vitamin pills. The pills may keep us alive, but they are not nurturing our whole beings, our senses and our integrative health.

The same is true of restricting our connections to the world to only the ways today's technology affords us; to only interacting in a cyber-reality. This is a way that can bring us closer together, but also may create a bigger distance between each other. We disconnect from our own senses in such relationships—not being aware of the other person's smell or body language. Such an interaction happens with less integrity than when we create a relationship person-to-person.

There are signs of hope and growing reasons for optimism, though. People are beginning to investigate a more organic way of living, including accelerated research into electro-_ magnetic vibrations and their effect on manifestation of our reality. The Vortex of

Energy Meditation, one of the three main pathways in the DHARMI Map that I will be discussing in another book, La Voie de la resonance, supports you to clarify, balance and strengthen your electro-magnetic field.

Despite the disheartening reckless consummation of energy and vital materials and the ever-increasing pace in our society, there is hope. There are ever more movements for peace, consciousness of the need for meditation and scientific discovery of healing properties in natural plants. Additional practitioners of yoga are stepping forward every day and concern with organic, locally sourced food and consumption of healthy meals has become a priority for many.

A Qigong instructor taught me that these days we need to boost our immune system twice as much as we needed to do in days past. Why? Because our systems are assailed by contamination in the food we eat, the water we drink and the air we breathe. We also subject our senses to overstimulation, by the constant gathering of information from the internet and the 24-hour-news cycle. We expose ourselves to radiation through constant use of computers, smartphones and other mobile devices. We are strongly influenced and affected by such toxins and dangerous stimulants in our own daily lives.

We also live in a world of credit cards, where we may get anything we want, immediately, whether we can afford it or not. This can preserve and support the growth and cultures, when used in a proper, moderated way. Though under some conditions, it can also overwhelm the process of growth and affect food grown with hormones, losing its natural substance or taste.

We receive tons of information and our attention is constantly drawn to the external factors and material things we need to be happy. We have been programmed since kindergarten to strive for the house, the mother and the dad, the two children and the dog, just as in our childhood drawings.

Yet is that the picture that will really make us happy? Perhaps that picture causes strong expectations, distancing us from the experience we can create within. Perhaps we have different dreams or paths. Perhaps we can find happiness in our own way within that same picture or within our own picture and realization.

Happiness is not only what we have—the newer, bigger, more expensive status symbol of the moment, the biggest house, the fastest car. Happiness instead is a way of living, a reflection of tuning into our hearts and nurturing healthy relationships.

I have noticed that many times when people focus on having more and wanting more, they begin to suffer from a lack. The more work, the less time. The more toys, the less opportunities to play. The more money, the less security. The more business, the less freedom. It is a matter of choice, direction and priorities for everyone in their own time.

We live in a world of fast food, though it can barely be called food, based as it is on meat raised with hormones and vegetables whose very cells have been substituted with genetically modified ingredients. How can our body ingest and assimilate those ingredients? Much the same as our overworked brains, like a sky covered with clouds, and contamination where we cannot see the path with clarity anymore, they can't process all the information with which they are barraged constantly. We live in a world of overpopulation and overconsumption, of dazzling wealth and dire poverty, of fertile jungles and arid deserts, of places overrun with non-native plants strangling the life out of the plants which nature placed there, of predators out of balance with their prey leading to species decimation, a world in which the natural cycles of creation are constantly being challenged. There is a time for rain and for tsunamis. There are times of dryness. It is part of nature, and so we, as human beings, naturally pass through different emotional states. There are times of heat, others of cold, such as when our motivation is engaged, when we feel the burn of the Fire Element. At other times, our Fire is at rest.

Yet, it is true that this time we live in is part of our evolution, as a planet and a people. People have access to extensive information and tools to become more conscious in many different fields and forms. This is a time of awakening.

People are noticing and receiving strong signals; alarms about possible disasters; threats to our well-being and our planet's well-being. Many are trying to reconnect, to re-center, to reflect and to become more mindful. They are searching for the power needed to survive this critical time. Meditation is now a must in order to re-center and clarify our minds—minds that are overwhelmed by an excess of information, overexcitement and constant stimulation seemingly coming from everywhere.

Active meditation to strengthen the electro-magnetic field is required in order to resist all the radiation and intense contamination from our environment. I describe a meditation you may use, called the Vortex of Energy Meditation in my book, La Voie de la Resonance.

In earlier times, we structured our lives around the changes of the seasons. These days we artificially try to control the seasons and complain bitterly when our carefully constructed thermostats and walls can't keep the power from blowing out, the snow off the roads or the hurricane from our shores. We try to master time and natural changes instead of realizing they are part of our world and part of our necessary experience.

In earlier times, we ate the local honey from our resident bees, sharing part of what they had created. Now, those bees are dying and we have to look farther afield for products like our honey. Much honey shipped from abroad lacks the properties to strengthen us with pollen from local plants and boost our immune system against allergies. Many people who greet the day by eating a spoon full of local raw honey find this can help cure their allergies. They breathe better and their respiration grows stronger. Now honey shipped from afar, over-processed and stripped of its healthful properties, is said to cause botulism in infants under the age of two. Why did we endanger local bees and continue a pattern of devaluing the wonderful things put here to aid us and make our lives easier and healthier? Why do we not see and be grateful for all the gifts we have been given? The gifts are all within and around us.

The Cycle through the Elements will remind you of your rhythms and your needs as human being. This level of consciousness brings the pieces of the puzzle together. It supports your journey to harmony and balance. It helps you to clarify your point of reference, to fill up the empty places within you and respond to your needs.

Many times we may intuitively know there are unfulfilled aspects within us. For lack of tools and education in that field, we may try frantically to fill them with things from outside—more food, more sex, more money, more work—pouring coals on the fires of ill health, loneliness, insecurity and a never-ending sense of feeling 'less than'. Some people continue to feel empty because the things with which they try to fill themselves up are substituting for what they really lack or need.

This is like being awash in emotions and sensations, like a flood of the water washing over us, causing us to lose our sense of control (Fire), our direction (Air) and our connectedness with our roots (Earth). It's like sitting down to a bountiful banquet and only eating dessert, without considering what your body needs at the time. Learning to listen to our needs, to our true calling, is fundamental, in order to respond with mindfulness and harmony.

The Five Elements and The Cycle through the Elements remind you of the fundamental and truly important aspects of your life's journey. It reminds you to consider all aspects of life as sacred and honorable.

It is a noble path, allowing abundance, acceptance, compassion and gratitude to take root and grow into a lush garden, the paths of which you can learn to navigate with grace, no matter who you are and no matter what transitions life has in store for you.

The Cycle through the Elements

This pathway leads you on a journey to take into consideration a holistic approach based on the Elements in all form of expression and realization.

The Cycle through the Elements can be worked in a full circle or in a one-way direction. Consider the flow of energy coming from above and/or from below you. You may be struck by a sudden revelation or vision. You may become inspired by something you hear or see or someone you meet or even have a dream that you know you have to act upon when you awaken. Any of these instances can help lead towards the manifestation. The flow of energy from below is revealed when you feel a

longing, a lack, a need or feel propelled to fulfill an obligation or compelled to accept a responsibility. Any of these instances push you forward towards a liberation, release or sense of fulfillment.

We have the possibility to bring clarity, to draw inspirations into our everyday life. We can actually nurture the earth, the community, and uplift the vibration of the planet to a higher vibration. We have the potential to become co-creator, to tune in with the drum, the very pulse of life felt within us by the beating of our heart. By joining our rhythm with other like-minded hearts, we can shake the very heavens and help manifest a new life here on earth.

In the DHARMI practice, consideration, compassion and clarity as expressed towards others, ourselves and the environment, is fundamental to the philosophy. We can learn to fulfill our responsibility and balance all aspects of both our exterior life (material, personal, familial, social, professional and cultural) and our interior life (physical, emotional, energetic, psychological and spiritual).

The tools that you will learn in these next chapters will awaken and free your creativity. The Elements provide you with a holistic approach, supporting your search for a healthy lifestyle and helping you in the manifestation of your ideas.

The Cycle through the Elements allows the integration (in a holistic way) of our intention, vision and purpose into our life. It shows the way to align and clarify parts of ourselves— like intelligence memory, emotional memory, self-esteem and cell memory. It gives tools to access to our own truth so that we might live a life with love and balance.

This pathway can be processed through reflection, visualization and meditation focused on healing, centering and self-development. It can also be used to clarify certain ideas and for decision-making or creation of a project or vision that you would like to manifest. By accessing both your exterior and interior aspects through the pathway and cycle, you can make use of the complementing factors of each, to reach your creative goal.

Here are some often-asked questions, you might find helpful, about The Cycle through the Elements:

What are the key aspects of The Cycle through the Elements?

It is important to be aware of the relationship between the Elements in our lives. Present situations or stories may inhibit the flow of energy, which can create stress. Using The Cycle through the Elements, it is possible to observe where there may be a resistance in the flow and create the opportunity for liberation through awareness. It can be applied internally to empower an intention in the Five Elements, as well as externally to bring an idea or project into manifestation.

How can this level of consciousness support my evolution?

I am aware of the flow of energy between the Elements in my life and I have been fortunate enough to be able to release blockages with mindfulness. With The Cycle through the Elements, I am able to investigate my inner state at any time and listen to the messages. Also, I use this tool to bring ideas to manifestation by

passing them through the Elements with creativity and consideration of each step.

How do I integrate the Cycle through the Elements into the Map and Cycle of Evolution?

The Cycle through the Elements can be used in Step 1 of the Cycle of Evolution to see where there may be a resistance in your personal flow; in Step 2 to observe the reaction; in Step 3 to align an intention or gift with the Elements; in Step 4 to embody a new role and see if it resonates in your life; and in Step 5 to integrate a new perspective. The meditations are especially useful here as they shed light on the balance between the Elements of Air, Fire, Water, Earth, and Ether.

How does the pathway benefit and support people's self- or professional development?

When people become aware of their life's flow, they are able to navigate the waves and surrender to what is. The cycle supports people to lasso an idea or inspiration and bring it down to manifestation. Also, we can make something happen with whatever resources are available to us in order to transform our situation. With a greater understanding of this cycle, we have a clear structure to follow as we are guided to channel our efforts with intention.

In many practices and philosophies, the various practitioners must go through things they are affected by mainly from exterior forces. They must make some external change—their job, their partner or their geographical location. However, such changes don't always support transition within, where it really counts. If a person continues with the same perspective and points of reference, they will attract the same people and things to their life and be attracted to similar situations, including those that caused the conflict or stress previously.

The Map addresses those vicious cycles in our life stemming from our core beliefs that act as an attractant to those unwelcome situations or unhealthy responses to certain situations. We can learn from the journey we take armed with the Map, to act from a space of unconditional surrender, without expectation of any return. When we act from a space of love, we experience love. When we are proactive and create a beautiful perspective, we see and experience life from that point of reference.

When we approach life from a clear intention, and honor healthy values, a natural selection begins to happen around us. We may see opportunities that we didn't see before. We may contain and direct ourselves with mindfulness, instead of rushing into familiar conflicts or stressful conditions that were enabling or feeding a specific pattern.

You invite a healthy response and clarifying influence to support your external manifestations. This reflects the decision to take your own responsibility for your life and distance yourself from a role of victim within yourself, your community and the world-at-large.

CHAPTER TWO
The Elements on the Journey

When I began to study holistic therapies, I was not aware that this foundation and these teachings could be applied to most aspects of our lives.

In this chapter, I will share with you how we can integrate the language and wisdom of nature into our life's perception and realization.

To do this, I continue to refer to the Five Fundamental Elements of Earth, Water, Fire, Air, and Ether.

These Elements, in relationship with each other, allow the manifestation of our mission and our visions. They animate our relationships with others and with our impermanent environment. As we connect with the different properties of these energies, we can explore how to use each Element as a tool for realization and expression.

The position of each Element is relative to the context of that which you are observing. For example, the physical body is the Earth in relation to our whole being. Yet, the Elements affect even more specialized parts of our body such as the digestive system, which is in relation to the Element of Water when we consider the Five Elements in the physical body.

Another example is the thoughts, which are the Air Element in relation to the whole being, even though the emotional response we think of is the influence of the Water Element in relation to the whole mind-spirit connection.

The quality of leadership, for instance, is mainly centered in the Fire Element. But leadership is made up of many skills, including emotional intelligence (affected by Water) and the ability to think clearly and long-term (affected by the Element of Air).

This introduction to the Five Elements will help you understand what the Elements are and how I see them helping you through integration into your life.

The Element of Earth—Form

This Element deals with all that nurtures and grounds us. It requires that we discipline ourselves to take care of our earthly form and that we access vital energy to keep ourselves strong and energized and thus capable of manifestation.

You need to tap your inner strength and ascertain how much vital energy you possess. The Earth will and does support and nurture you every day, unconditionally. Contact with the Earth Element will empower you. When you enter into connection with Mother Earth, direct contact with that Element in nature will deepen the experience of being nurtured and supported.

This Element feeds our basic needs; the ones that trigger the urge to create, to procreate and to manifest. It is the foundation and support that allows the manifestation of inspiration and ideas turning them into matter, into physical form.

A strong discipline and clear organization helps us to grow. When the foundation is well- organized, just as when a garden is well-nurtured, the planted seeds will grow and our garden will thrive.

First, of course, we need to have the right soil and growing conditions, so that our seeds will thrive, but we also need intention. What do we expect from our garden? It is the same when we consider our own needs. We must examine if the soil in which we hope to manifest our dreams is fertile and discover its condition (physical, economic and environmental). Will the seeds we plan to plant (our intentions) find the garden a nurturing place, a safe place to grow and lift their faces to the sun? We need to examine and clarify, and then follow, step-by-step, the garden plan that will give our plants the best chance to grow.

No matter what we lack to get what we need (money, resources, information), we must make use of the Earth Energy to provide what we need to not only survive and not just survive, but thrive. Through research and creativity, we can use this Energy to create what we lack. The energy called into play by the Earth Element is sacred and valuable with great power to help provide the resources we need.

Through the process, you can empower your connection to the energy of the earth. You will discover how much vital current you possess. You will receive answers about how much this power is influencing you and the people around you.

Physically, the Earth is the structure and base of your body. From a holistic point of view, the Earth relates to prosperity and the way we deal with our survival needs like food, nutrition, money, sex and basic hygiene. It is about the call to know where you stand, to create a family, to build a house, to own properties, to 'have'. Some people feel always a lack, feeling unsafe and fearing loss.

We are creatures of habit. A small change in our routine can be experienced as an earthquake. A big shift related to our family, to our work, to our location or status, can be the source of a deep metamorphosis, and, as such, serve to enlighten and help us create.

The Element of Water—Flow

This Element deals with our emotions and our emotional intelligence. Both, of course, strongly affect our relationships.

How do you deal with relationships and daily emotional pressure? The connection with the Water Element supports you to manage stress and channel the flow of your emotions, which liberates your life flow.

Satisfying relationships and awareness are key aspects for a balanced life. We awaken emotions and influence our surroundings when we create. We are also very influenced by our environment and relationships. Healthy values will support healthy relationships. The clearer the Water, the more harmonious the flow and the communication.

The Water Element balances the Fire Element; while the Fire supports the control and direction, Water directs the expression of our emotions. A clear perception and healthy sensibility support us to bring harmony and grace to our actions. But Water also requires a container from which to flow. We find it in the Earth Element, which provides discipline, stability and support.

The Water Element is directly linked to our emotions and how we process life's experiences. Notice whether you react to particular emotions from a space of resistance, pressure or flow. Our connection with Water, especially the ocean, releases us from stress and liberates our life's flow.

Physically, Water reflects the stomach area and digestive system. The manifestation of the Water Element can be seen by an inflammation, an excess or lack of fat, or retention of Water.

Emotional intelligence is the ability to identify, assess, and control our emotions and those of others. There are four types of abilities: Perceiving emotions, using emotions, understanding emotions and managing emotions.

Our emotional memory influences us strongly in our perceptions, in our creativity and in our relationships.

The Element of Fire—Shine

The Fire Element has to do with movement, direction, our self-esteem and leadership.

How do you direct your actions? Are you sensitive to your feelings? Active meditation focusing on the sun and Fire will bring you more energy and warmth.

Our interactions and expression reflect our level of creativity, inspiration, confidence and awakening. We need to develop a healthy self-esteem and find confidence in ourselves, to honor our values and to stay true to our path.

We cannot find determination, act with clarity or engage ourselves into any direction when we lack self-confidence. Being too wishy-washy doesn't help to grow. Even so, not everyone feels the desire to practice leadership in his or her life. That choice is perfectly fine. We all have our priorities. We all have our role in the society.

Whether it is an improvisation or a role that has been studied or developed after much research, the flame shines, moves and affects everyone who sees its glow. We can therefore only hide a creation for a limited time. The seed grows to finally appear out of the earth. It becomes visible. It appears and is exposed to judgment, to external conditioning. It cannot be denied—it is the expression of the Fire.

Fire evokes the energy, direction and motivation to move forward with enthusiasm. Physicality, pulsation, movement and musculature reflect Fire. You can access the Fire within, nurture it, harness it and unleash more of who you truly are. The flame within us can bring warmth and support our actions and relationships. It burns, it moves, it shines.

There are even Fire Elementals, salamanders, which reside in campfires, woodstoves or anywhere there is a fire. They thrive near the flames. So can we. With the Fire, you act, move and shape yourself, your expression and your life.

When the fire is overactive, it can burn itself and others. This will be shown by a passion that may be very strong, but short. People so affected may overdo, use up too much of their energy. Sometimes their actions are the reflection of an overflow of emotions. Then the Fire is extinguished as the passion within us may be. We can learn to nurture the flame within us to support the direction of our actions. There is a way to relate to the Fire Element, making use of its offered warmth and positive energy.

The Element of Air—Clarity

The Air Element deals with mindfulness, reflection and breath.

How do your belief systems and thoughts support or limit you? The sacred breath and fresh Air bring you clarity and peace.

Our mind is free, yet it is clearer when we give it direction, lightness, and space. A sense of reflection is key for all creation. There is a thought and idea behind all manifestation.

The Air invites us to pursue an idea, to linger over a thought, to clarify a dream, to allow for inspiration. It's the antenna that captures and then transmits the messages. The breeze and the fresh Air bring us clarity and peace. Air relates to the ways that our belief system dictates our decisions. How we judge or perceive each situation can directly affect the outcome.

The skin and the breath represent the Air on the physical level. Air is associated with Elemental Beings, called sylphs, whom we may call upon to help us work with this Element.

In this Air, we develop the adult within us; we explore different perspectives and our own minds. We examine our culture and affirm or deny some beliefs, setting parameters in our thoughts. Our perspective is created by our core beliefs and proved true or not by our learning experience. This knowledge is stored in our four other Elements as we think through our experiences. All of our observations and reflections are based on our perspective and judgment.

The Air can capture an overflow of ideas and thoughts that can be overwhelming to the other Elements and limit the progress of manifestation. A strong judgment or core belief can cause a stress and prevent the person from receiving any new ideas. He or she won't be receptive to new possibilities.

A balanced Air Element will allow a clear selection and reflection through life's journey.

The clarification of an affirmation or mantra will support the flow of creativity, clearing, aligning and integrating all the Elements.

The Element of Ether—Essence

The Element of Ether deals with our intention, the vital energy (qi in Chinese philosophy, prana in yoga philosophy) and how well we integrate cosmic intelligence. It also concerns the DNA from our ancestors—our personal Tree of Life.

How aligned are you with cosmic intelligence and the source of creation? A space for meditation and inspiration is made with Ether, which forms the connection of all the Elements within one.

We receive inspiration from the space, from our dreams, from something we see, hear, feel or perceive. When we are in the zone, we have an unrestricted open perception that goes beyond the linear thinking process—literally transcending the mind.

In this Element, we find the sense of liberation through surrender, detachment and eventual connection. We have come to the heart of the matter, the core of our sacred beings. The Ether is source of inspiration, is where there are infinite possibilities and we can experience a limitless expansion.

Of the Five Elements, the Ether is the energy that connects us all. The magnetic field around our body recognizes positive or negative vibrations in our surroundings. We are blessed when we connect with this magnetic energy.

We often know things without knowing how we know. In other words, we are inspired by a Higher Purpose. The connection of all within one appears in moments of meditation. When we are conscious of the etherical field, we honor the unknown, the mystery of life. It is a space for wisdom, perception, and most importantly, faith.

This level of consciousness reminds us the sacredness of every moment, of every being on this earth, of all within and around us. Ether is the medium through which we feel a connection to the source of creation. It is also the space where we are alert to synchronicities. It is the Source Essence.

The Four Pillars

The Four Pillars: physical strength, emotional, psychological, and energetic, when added to purpose, intention, frequency, and spirituality, equal the Five Elements.

We all use the Four Pillars throughout our lives as keys to growth. They are ways to reach objectives, and to transcend limitations and reach liberation.

The Four Pillars are the keys that built the pyramids and temples that have lasted thousands of years. They can build lasting things in your life as well. They are the foundation for all that we want to manifest. They are the channels to bring spirit or a vision into matter.

Just as a seed needs the Elements, the seed which is the intention or Ether, the fertile soil of the Earth, the Water to nurture, the sun or Fire to warm and the Air in order to grow, we human beings need to use and balance the Four Pillars in the process of manifestation. Directing our thoughts in a way that nurtures our intention is opening the field in other dimensions. If your vision is to live in abundance, your thoughts and words will be orientated from that healthy space. You won't communicate from a space of want, lack and misery, instead you will express yourself from a confident space, acknowledging what you have, looking at possibilities, and growing from there.

The First Pillar is a vision or inspiration from which we align our thoughts. This is the psychological aspect of the Four Pillars.

The Second Pillar is the energetic aspect, that which motivates us to put our lives in motion. Your actions through the day will be directed towards this vision and intention with motivation. Your actions will reflect abundance and this will project confidence.

The Third Pillar is the emotional aspect, which inspires us to share and support each other with healthy values and harmony.

The Fourth Pillar is the physical realm, wherein you will strengthen the foundation and create space and time for the manifestation of the vision.

We need a clear intention, a purpose that motivates us to activate and focus on these pillars. Also we have to balance and strengthen the Four Pillars in order to experience and to manifest our intention. These forces are intertwined. They complement each other. We can learn how to use all four for our greater good and for the good of our environment.

CHAPTER THREE
Elements for Holistic Self-Development

This chapter presents the main aspects in which we can integrate the Elements for holistic self-development.

Healthy lifestyle and well-being

Relationships and emotional intelligence

Self-esteem and leadership

Mindfulness and Stress management

Navigating life transitions

You will notice that each of those elementals aspects in our life are taking into consideration a subcategory related to each Element. This process reveals how they are all intertwined and complement each other.

Key Elements for a Healthy Lifestyle: Living With Well Being—Earth Element

Release stress and cultivate a healthy lifestyle. Whether at home in your daily routine, or in the office, a holistic and integrated approach to your life is possible. When balancing the Elements, nurturing and giving the proper attention to all of them, you will find your way to a balanced and healthy lifestyle. The key is proper organization and discipline, with enough flexibility to allow you to grow.

Certain Elements are essential for balancing your well-being. When your lifestyle is out of balance, you will receive signs that manifest physically and emotionally. Rest is an important aspect to which we should pay attention.

We all need time to rest, to integrate, to resource ourselves. Consider such time as vital to digest and assimilate the experiences and thoughts that bombard us. Learn to care for your basic need for rest with gentle discipline, while incorporating healthier sleep patterns. In our busy lives, we may be driven by a restless rhythm of activities and intellectual stimulations. We resist the nighttime, using lights, noise, television and our countless screens to divert us from our need to rest. We distance ourselves from our inner peace and center. We are trying to make up for things we didn't have enough time to finish during the day or divert our busy thoughts with some entertaining distraction. We stay up too late and then feel too tired when we awaken in the morning and start the cycle once again. Our whole system and inner clock are unbalanced.

Why do we resist nature's rhythm? In the society in which we live, there is little space for quality time. We have a tendency to forget the inhale, the exhale, the pause. Here we could learn from the best musicians, who know how to play that pause.

We can best receive and integrate the food we eat when we give a space and time for our digestive system to process what we've eaten. Instead of choosing fast food as opposed to carefully chosen quality organic ingredients and rushing through our meal with no attention paid to chewing carefully, savoring the flavors and only eating enough so that we are sated, we grab the nearest drive-through burger, throw it down our throats while checking our email and eat it all negligently. That is no way to honor our bodies.

Having a good discipline in life, respecting healthy boundaries, and organizing your time in a functional way to allow yourself to rest provides you a healthy grounded foundation, from which you can grow. This is the Element of Earth at work.

Do you experience stress in relationship to your body and nutrition?

Nurture your body with proper alimentation, by being sensitive to your body's needs. Most of the food we eat comes from our emotional body, the 'hungry ghost' that we have within us. How many times do you eat something because of a sensation you are looking for, an emotional connection you have with a specific food. Often it is not the best for you at this time, yet, it responds to the voice of the hungry ghost—that part of you that says, "Eat that" because you saw a commercial and the dish looked good, "Eat this," because this candy bar will make you feel less sad or "Eat that" entire bowl of popcorn to fill the empty space inside you. We eat some food in response to an emotional trigger, such as the food we received as a child to comfort us. This is the very meaning of 'comfort food'—yet you find, in the end, it truly gives no comfort as it is not what you need at this time. It takes attention to listen attentively and respond to the call from within.

You may feel guilty when you eat or rush. The relationship you create with the food, and the way you eat is as important as what you eat. If you are mindful in your eating patterns, you can reassess your relationship with the food, with your body and with your emotions. When we become more sensitive to ourselves, we also are more sensitive of our environment. This is the Element of Water in play.

Do you lack motivation to move, or find good excuses not to exercise?

Incorporating exercise that fits your needs and movement that responds to your bioenergy rhythm can vibrantly uplift your energy.

We live in a time where everything is rushed. We are all influenced by our surroundings and are driven by influences of the media, the internet and a lifestyle of conspicuous consumption. It may be difficult to resist such drives, excitements and aspects that feed an unhealthy ego. Many people, by following their own restless rhythms are spinning their wheels, very busy doing nothing rather than just actually doing nothing— like resting or reflecting.

I have met many people who are distracted by always doing things, but not the things that will bring them any closer to fulfilling their own desires or realizing their own dreams. The flame within us gets weaker as we go along in such a fashion, until we redirect our actions and our behaviors towards something more in tune with our true inner-calling. Sometimes our need for external encouragement and recognition leads to a lack of confidence and prevents us from pursuing our dreams.

Regular exercise, moving our body, dancing until we find that clear, pure connection with our heart, our rhythm and our own dance steps in life, will help us begin to unveil those steps day-by-day. Bringing awareness to our behaviors and actions will influence our well-being and the well-being of our environment.

This is the Element of Fire being used intentionally and mindfully in our lives.

Do you have difficulty breathing? Are your thoughts often distressing? Breathe deeply, and clarify your mind with clear intention.

We receive so much information daily. We are over-programmed and can lose clarity in our reflections. We are so influenced by all the excess of consciousness, bombarded with facts, opinions and noise that we may be unable to practice mindfulness.

Can we still breathe, still clarify our thoughts and vision in this maze of often-conflicting information? Many lose their own perspective and opinion, having their mind brainwashed by media personalities or calculated public relations campaigns. Our serenity may be lost by exposure to constant bad news and violent video games. Our thinking gets scattered. We can lose focus and attention easily. Proper intellectual stimulation and learning to concentrate our thinking, helps develop a strong mind.

Bringing awareness to our breath and observing our thought process, gives us the opportunity to reenter and clarify our mind. It helps give us some space, a certain distance from our instant reaction, giving us time to respond responsibly. Such are the gifts of the Element of Air.

Is there a specific aspect of your life or health that you avoid facing or dealing with?

Some aspects of our life are not within our control. Yet we can learn to practice acceptance and continue living our lives with compassion, harmony and inspiration.

There are aspects of our lives, such as the aging, that are part of our natural evolution. If we resist this natural flow, it is more stressful and resisting requires us to spend a lot of unnecessary energy. Yet, it is possible to age gracefully, accepting what is and doing the best to get the most out of our life's experiences, integrating the wisdom that we have awakened along the journey. As long as we try to change things and struggle with what is, we keep spinning in a whirlpool of stress and unfulfilled expectations.

For example, are you short and you would like to be taller? Since this cannot be, how does it help to resist your reality, to judge yourself badly? Such resistance will only make you smaller and smaller in spirit through your days. Making peace with what is, is the best way to open the doors to new possibilities and development.

Such acceptance and surrender is the essence of the Element of Ether.

A healthy foundation allows us to support the manifestation of our inspirations and dreams. When we rest well, eat well, move well, and breathe well, we notice how wonderful it feels to feel good. The Map helps you find your way towards a balanced and healthy lifestyle, tailored to your needs and priorities.

When I lived in Buenos Aires, a woman named Dominica came to see me to find more balance in her life. She was passing through a difficult time with a hectic schedule with her children and her work.

She also began putting on weight and that was adding to her stress. She tried different diets, but none of them was working for her.

Her relationship with the food was not very good. She liked sweets a lot and always felt guilty or angry with herself after eating them. She had very scattered eating habits. Sometimes she skipped a meal, even when she felt hungry, and then ate too much later to try to compensate. She was repressing her own desires with sugar rushes.

She didn't have much time to exercise or enjoy any hobbies and she shared that she was feeling very tired. She could sleep very deeply, though she didn't feel that she was resting well.

We took some time to review her organization and lifestyle. With a clear perspective, she began to organize her thoughts and priorities. She could set a schedule of when to eat and allow some time to give space for things she liked to do.

We began to create a few clear points of reference in the middle of her hectic and busy schedule. As she began to be more sensitive to her well-being and to the foods she chose to nourish her body, she was more attracted to fruits, vegetables and whole grains. She noticed that her craving for sweets was diminished.

She made the adjustments a little at a time, step-by-step, to allow a harmonious transition. We took into consideration her family, work schedule, as well as her personal needs.

A few weeks after we began our work together, she told me that she was losing weight without dieting. As her body and mind became more focused and clear, and as her actions became more directed, her digestion improved and she felt more energized.

The rhythms and directions you include on your Map may work very well at a certain time of your life. However, it is best to review your Map regularly and do fine tuning of alignments and make changes if needed.

These kinds of changes, such as those of diet, will best be made during certain times, when your body calls out for good nutrition to meet its physical needs. At other times, such as during vacation when your most ambitious plans call for you lay on the beach all day, your needs will be different. That doesn't mean you can throw all your newfound balance out the window on vacation. You still should respect your need for a balanced lifestyle and harmonious rhythm, but you can tinker with your diet a bit, maybe incorporating local dishes and regional cuisine and add exercise by trying out something new and fun like scuba diving or skiing. Being ever mindful of trying for your strong foundation, balance and maintaining your points of reference can help you have a better and more fulfilling experience, both while you are on vacation and in your daily life.

I worked with Anne, who was experiencing constant anxiety and struggle in her life. She was working overtime and felt like she was running in circles, with no time for herself or space to truly live. She couldn't find the energy to exercise or to organize her home. When she finished work, she was so stressed that she could think of nothing better to do than to share a few drinks with co-workers who gathered at a local bar to complain about their own unhappy circumstances. Such gatherings and company did nothing to lift Anne's spirits or help her out of her predicament.

Anne added a little exercise to her everyday routine. Next she took her hour-long lunch break off-site, away from her workplace. This worried her at first. She was convinced that she could lose her job and that her absence would seem to her boss as though she wasn't devoted enough to her work, responsibility or position.

Yet, Anne found the opposite was true. Not only did she keep her job, but because of allowing herself the mental break, she became even more productive.

At home, Anne began to explore different hobbies and interests. She remembered that she always wanted to dance. So she began to take dance classes two times a week in the evening. She found herself looking forward to her classes and became a happier person.

When she began to be more sensitive to her needs and allowed herself more space, she also changed her eating habits. Her senses were more alert and she found herself choosing foods of higher quality and better nutrition.

In just a few weeks, Anne's perspective shifted and she began to practice a more balanced lifestyle. These slight adjustments also inspired other people around her to try and incorporate such changes in their own lives. She was helping others just by her good example. When I saw Anne again a few months ago, she had much to report. She had gotten a promotion, was sleeping better and now had a much better quality of life.

Emotional Intelligence and Relationships: Considering the Flow of Emotions
Water Element

We are all constantly influenced by internal and external triggers and our emotions are sensitive to movements and thoughts.

Our emotions can be overwhelming and, sometimes, difficult to channel. Sometimes we repress certain emotions and, at other times, in other situations, we experience bursts of emotions. We may judge these emotions as either good or bad. Emotions are only emotions and we can direct them into positive or negative expressions, into positive or negative feelings. But we feel best when we experience our emotions unconditionally, channeling them creatively. They are part of our emotional body, our reality, whether we like them or not. Learning to relate to them, channel them with intention and use them as a spur for creative expression can be very productive and beneficial to ourselves and our environment.

Emotions and relationships are like water. Just as water drops blend together and form an ocean, then evaporate into the clouds to fall again as rain drops, sometimes we people get very close to each other, and sometimes we need space.

Our emotions are constantly changing—it is part of our nature. Dealing with these constant changes can be difficult, and can even become a struggle in some circumstances.

We do have different levels of relationships, and sometimes we get confused whether someone fits into our life as only a colleague or as a close friend or more, as lover and partner. These roles are dynamic, moving like waves, and may change and then change back again. The more we resist those natural fluctuations, the more breakable our relationships and we become. If we try to 'freeze' and hold onto a specific relationship, we can lose the flow and the space for both to grow together. Attachments, conditions and expectations are hurtful for the emotional body. They block the flow and limit the clarity, truth, and creative expression. Yet, the commitment to healthy values, as well as honoring your truth and emotional boundaries, gives you the tools to channel your emotions with respect and clarity in your relationships. That is when the feelings come into consideration. The emotional body is directly linked with our vital energy, and it is our responsibility to develop the skills and ways to contain that energy and direct it with a positive intention, and healthy values.

I invite you to consider the Five Elements, as integrated into different forms of relationships:

Your responsibility for yourself includes your thoughts and the air you breathe (Element of Air), your inspirations and feelings (Element of Fire), your emotions (Element of Water), your body (Element of Earth) and your path (Element of Ether).

Your relationship with your surroundings includes your family, friends, cultural and social environment, your professional team, spiritual tribe and community.

In this holistic approach, I am considering five main levels of relationships. In a specific relationship, we may relate to all five, or we may relate only on one or a few levels.

In the Air Element, I consider like-minded people. The relationships that you create at cultural events, or at the university or with others engaged in study on some kind. It is a level that is mainly intellectual. You share ideas, concepts, and perspectives. You support each other's reflections, perspectives, interests, and cultural development.

In the Fire Element, I consider the people you relate with while sharing hobbies, as well as those that serve to motivate and inspire each other to grow and to develop both of your potentials. You find some people on this level complementing you and others with whom you find challenges. The main intention in these relationships is to uplift each other, to nurture a healthy self-esteem and to build self-confidence. This level may include professional relationships also, if your profession is aligned with your vision, makes use of your main talent and develops your potential.

In the Water Element, I consider the close friends, people with whom you get together to hang out and share quality time. It is people with whom you can play. Remember the best friends with whom you played in the sandbox? Those were among the first people outside of your family with whom you learned to feel emotionally involved. These people exert a strong influence on you and whom you can influence as well and with whom you feel very connected at an emotional level. These are the people with whom you can share your ups and down, laugh and cry together, be happy and sometimes angry. You feel as though you can lift the burden from your shoulders, close your eyes, and flow. Some of the closest friends give you the opportunity to feel supported and accepted emotionally.

In the Earth Element, I consider the family and intimate relationships—those people with whom you are very close. You have a sense of belonging. You come from your family; they are your foundation. There is a profound level of commitment to each other. You support each other. That is when you can say "my" child, "my" family, "my" husband; the ones that are so close it feels like they are part of you. They are part of your life and you are part of theirs, with a strong level of commitment.

In the Ether Element, we consider a community and our spiritual relationship. It is the agape love relation, fully unconditional. The people you include in this level of relationship are all those you can love, free of attachment or any expectation. It is a love that doesn't require any physical or material exchange, not even a word or exchange in the other dimensions. This is the sensation you have when you meditate, relate, visualize, and connect with the community and/or a specific vibration you like to sync with or tune into.

When you are clear about the level of relationship, you can deal better with emotional space or boundaries. This doesn't mean imposing emotional limitations, but rather a healthy selectiveness to support the clarity and flow in your emotional well-being, balance and growth.

As I wrote previously, your place in the levels is dynamic and may change. For example, after a divorce, it is time to reconsider your communication and emotional space in the relationship with your former spouse. The person, with whom you shared so much intimacy and transparency, may now be a person with whom you will share mainly conversations and reflections, with more distance between you. This will be reflected in your body language, the way you say hello. The language and even tone of the voice will change as you adapt to this new relationship level. You are relating emotionally to the same person, yet the level of your relationship is now different.

The more you clarify your relationship, the better you can relate and care for your own sensibility and perception. It is your responsibility to manage your emotions and channel them with as much clarity as possible.

You can experience different levels of love in any of these levels of relationships. This is exemplified in the Greek Orthodox tradition, where they have four words to describe different levels of love:

Storge, which reflects the love one feels towards the family that may require some sacrifice and shows the aforementioned level of natural attachments, as in "my" child, "my" husband, "my" father.

Filia, which is the type of love that you feel for your friends, with the people with whom you share hobbies, interests, dreams and projects.

Eros, which is the passionate and intimate relationship that you have with your lover.

Agape, which is a love that is from an open heart, free, unconditional and spiritual. It is the sense of 'being in the state of love.'

Love can be an emotion, a feeling, a state of being or an intention. It all depends of the perspective and context in which you use the term 'love'. At its purest sense, it is All.

Some people and situations appear along our way and trigger diverse emotions. The influence from our surroundings can be strong, and make us react out of fear, anger, frustration, love, compassion or resentment. Many times, it will awaken memories or repressed emotions, giving us the chance to face and channel them with intention. Or the person may react to his or her past memories, even if he or she doesn't have any direct relation with the memory and no longer is in the emotional cycle that resulted in the reaction.

When we learn and channel our emotions and direct them, we can use the power to balance our relationships.

As you can see, when we speak about love, there are many definitions and forms of love. This is true of the other emotions as well. Everyone has a different interpretation, judgment and experience related to each emotion. For some people, as soon as they feel some anxiety, they block the emotion, judging it is bad to feel anxiety. Others are content to sit with the anxious emotion, waiting until it passes with patience and consideration, while others may channel this emotion creatively and with intention.

Some people even deal with such an emotion by grabbing something outside them to distract themselves from the anxiety. As children, they may have received a sweet as a way to calm down from an upset. They may grab for food during trying times as adults, also. Have you ever fed the 'hungry ghost', when, in reality, you were not actually physically hungry? We create so many eating habits that we are not listening to our bodies anymore or being sensitive to what would really give us a sense of being nurtured.

Everyone have a different way to relate to their emotions, and their response mechanism in different situations will reflect their own personal way to deal with them.

I have seen people become paralyzed in situations of conflict. When they feel anger or frustration, they block and try to repress that emotion. This can affect their health, as well as influence the type of people they will attract and be attracted to in their lives.

Others go into denial when it is time to face a difficulty. They are looking for an easy way out. They will try to lean on others to shoulder the burden. They won't take responsibility for their own actions.

Some people are enablers making sure that everyone is staying in their comfort zone. It can be a way to stay away from confrontation and to try to be accepted by their loved ones, or boss, or friends.

They are many forms and ways to respond to emotions, and this reflects in the way we relate with our surroundings, people and situations.

The same happens in our relationships. In many situations, and relationships, we have a tendency to create patterns that we continue to 'feed' continuously. Sometimes we fight over and over about a same subject that was bothering us and we can't seem to let go. We have created that response mechanism and the relationship is based on that dynamic. It takes courage and clarity to shift the way we relate with someone, while staying caring and trying to nurture the relationship. We may relate to that person from another perspective, emotional influence or dynamic.

Many relationships are manipulative, though that doesn't mean that the person wants to consciously manipulate others. There is a fine line between manipulation and influence. We are all influenced by each other's emotions, reactions, words and movements. Bringing awareness to the emotional intelligence and investing our emotional capital with positive intention requires a high level of attention, alertness and truth.

Being mindful of our emotions helps us notice when and how we are influenced. It gives us a chance to choose to follow that influence or to take another route that will be more in tune with our intention and honor our healthy boundaries.

Conflict or the sensation of being stuck in a relationship is one of the main causes of stress. It is an opportunity to listen to your emotional body. Observe the ways you respond, relate, and channel your emotions. Discover what this relationship or situation is triggering within you.

I believe that every emotion exists for a reason. We can try to think about emotions as other than simply good or bad or positive or negative. Emotions are directly linked to our vital energy. What make them positive or negative are our personal perspectives and the way we approach them. I encourage you to channel your emotions wisely, consciously and with intention.

Thus is possible as long as the emotions are waves that can be managed, and not tsunamis of intense fear, panic, pain and suffering, which we wouldn't be able to manage until they pass and we can reassess our direction.

Many times we respond from our emotional memory, even if it is not directly related to the present situation. Emotions and reactions may be triggered by a word, a thought, a smell or a piece of music. Often, we respond from our memories related to those trigger, from our pain body, past experiences, and belief systems—losing connection with the reality of the moment. The emotional memory is stored in the limbic system, the enteric nervous system, along with other fundamentals in the flow of emotions. I invite you to heal the emotional body. Develop the emotional intelligence with clarity, compassion, and direction.

Healthy relationships are the key to happiness. This doesn't have to mean being married, being in a romantic relationship or having many friends. This means having a healthy, good quality relationship with yourself, your loved ones, and your surroundings—feeling happy and in harmony.

You can manage your stress and heal wounds that may influence your reactions and your approach to certain level of relationships. Through this process, you will find your way towards healthy relationships.

Jake and Morgan, a couple in a romantic partnership, contacted me to help clarify the communication in their relationship. They felt stuck. Their intention was to find more harmony and allow their relationship to evolve and grow.

Both of them were coming from a different point of reference. Morgan had been married in the past, had a child with her husband, and later divorced. She then entered in a loving relationship with Jake and then, they had a child together.

Jake liked his freedom and independent way of being. He had an earlier relationship as well, though he didn't marry or have any children from his past relationship. He fell in love with Morgan and committed to a relationship with her and to building a family, but he felt some resistance to the idea of marrying.

Both Jake and Morgan had some resistance and fear in their partnership, mainly related to past experiences. They used their emotional capital to create and to evolve, yet, the aspect of commitment and engagement on the Earth (Storge) level of their relationship was difficult to accept. They were very much in love with each other. Their feelings (Fire) were very clear.

They agreed that they needed some time to process and nurture more emotional support between each other. Each needed to treat the other with more acceptance and compassion (Water). They also noticed that they needed to clarify some things between them (Air), including the expectations they had of each other. The more clearly they expressed themselves to each other, the more ease they could find. Then they were each better able to accept committing to each other and reaching another level of growth in their relationship. This naturally improved their family dynamic.

When they began to balance the Elements in their relationships, some synchronicities and new opportunities opened on their path. All was aligning, naturally, to point to that next step in their family-relationship. They married a few weeks later.

How Far Should We Go in a Relationship?

Claudia met one of her friends at the beach. He was with some others friends and invited Claudia to join them for a dinner. They were going to a restaurant close to her home. Usually, she was shy with strangers and would have begged off saying that she was too tired to join them and would rather have just gone home. But when she received this invitation, she was at a juncture in her life where she was trying to be more open and receptive—trying to say "yes" more often.

On the way to the restaurant, she was rethinking her decision to go with the group. Old fears and doubts, the basis for her shyness, came to the surface. Yet, she recognized that those thoughts were coming from the pain body and chose instead to focus on clearing her mind. Even that she was feeling very emotional, she met the group at the restaurant.

They were a group of four nice and fun men in their early forties. Her first thought was that they must be married or engaged, and were just having a "Guys Day Out". She joined a conversation about common interests and discovered that all the men were in fact single, like Claudia herself was. But she kept a careful eye on the men's behavior and had to admit they all treated her, the only woman present, with respect and consideration.

Claudia shared that she was going on a trip and was going to buy a highly-rated backpack. One of the men, Joe, was kind enough to offer to lend his own. He had no trips planned in the near future and said she shouldn't have to make such an expensive investment just for one trip.

Claudia's first reaction was to say "no". Yet she noticed this was just an old, knee-jerk defense mechanism, so she accepted his offer. She knew she was opening herself to get to know Joe better and that it would mean a second level in their friendship was beginning.

They kept in touch in the next few days and their communication was easy and flowing, Claudia and Joe agreed on a time to have her stop by to get the bag and, when she arrived, he had just finished cooking a gourmet meal.

Joe's kindness and openness were attractive to her. They also shared similar hobbies, such as cooking and yoga, and were even the same age. When he invited her to dinner, she stayed.

During the dinner conversation, Joe expressed his interest in beautiful, young women. Claudia, in her forties, paid attention to that fact, tried not to take it personally, and mentally recommitted to staying open to a friendship with him.

Joe, for his part, was very nice to Claudia, even asking why she wasn't married. She responded with a question of her own, asking him what he thought the reason was. His answer surprised her, "You look like you are very fulfilled and self-contained. A man wouldn't know what he could add into your life," Joe said. She thought about his statement later at home and wondered how she could appear so self-contained and yet, in truth, still be so shy.

After Claudia sent a text to thank Joe for dinner, they exchanged texts every now and again, but they didn't meet for more than a year. Each was on his or her own path.

Later on, they reconnected. Joe joined her for an event and they had a good time together. Claudia felt very attracted to him, but noticed his propensity for younger women. He even made a comment about her skin showing its age, and though he hadn't meant it to be insulting, the comment stung. Clearly he didn't have any physical or chemical attraction to her.

Their friendship grew in the next few weeks and months. They began to share more quality time together and became closer. Claudia had to stay in a clear communication space honoring what was fully present, respecting the reality of both of them, never overlooking herself and her own priorities.

One evening, Claudia and Joe went to a dinner with his friends. Afterwards, he invited her to his home to share a dessert. Claudia was tempted. She felt very attracted to him, but she chose to respect her values and to not cross a boundary that would lead to confusion and might affect their friendship in an unhealthy way. She used clarity, the Element of Air, in her communications and interactions with Joe.

They both had already spoken about what they are looking for in relationships. He was looking for a young, attractive woman whom he could marry and with whom start a family.

Claudia had been married in her thirties. She was now focusing her energy and attention on a vision that was very meaningful for her, one that involved a deeper involvement in her community. She would have been very happy to find a love partner, a companion who would love her for who she was and support her dreams and intentions as she would his, but getting married and having children were not part of her projected future anymore.

Despite the difference in the dreams they had for themselves, Claudia enjoyed their friendship and wanted to continue. But she knew that, had she crossed the boundary between them that night, their relationship might not have survived.

As it is, their friendship continues to grow. They respect each other and each values the relationship very much. Claudia still notices some emotional triggers when they relate by phone or in person. She honors this learning experience, choosing a path of consciousness, with open heart.

The tools that she has used with conscious communication supported her to lead her relationship with mindfulness. She, using the Element of Air, was aware of what they spoke about and worked hard at clarifying what she wanted and attentive to what he wanted. She recognized what motivated and inspired Joe and she to want to see each other. She tried her best to nurture a warm interaction, not allowing the flame to get too low, nor allowing it to burn out. She noticed that it was a two-way relationship, and that he was both responding and inviting (Fire). She recognized when some past or unhealthy emotions where triggered and could channel them wisely, using the Element of Water. She chose to respect a healthy distance (Earth), and noticed that this healthy distance allowed her to live more fully from the heart, making room for surprising synchronicities (Ether). Their relationship continues with healthy boundaries and has been one of the most inspiring friendships.

Life synchronicities have given Claudia and Joe a chance to travel together to different countries, share hobbies, and meet to inspire and support each other on their own paths.

When we apply conscious communication in our daily life, as they have, we become more aware of the synchronicities on our path. Consciousness and clarity support the alignment and manifestation of our intention. It nurtures a loving space in our heart and relationships. Honoring healthy values, as well as being compassionate and sensitive, gives us tools to recognize what level of relationship best suits different circumstances, people, and ourselves.

As you will read in the section dedicated to conscious communication, we do have a different body language and space between each other related to the level of relationship we share—whether it is between friends, colleagues, or in an intimate relationship.

Self-Esteem and Leadership

Making decisions with confidence while taking your feelings into consideration is utilizing the Fire Element. Choosing such decisive steps boosts our self-esteem and inspires confidence in our actions.

When we consider the Five Elements, we can make clearer decisions, ones that will be aligned with our priorities, needs, values, and inspirations of the moment. A good decision at a certain time of our life may reflect as a bad decision in another time. A direction may work well for someone, while it may not be so balanced for another person. It all depends of our intention, priorities, and values as well as our gifts, talents, and interests.

We can learn something new by exploring other ways and forms. If we do make a mistake, it is an opportunity for us to learn, to explore and to find a better way that will work best for us.

It is best to make new mistakes rather than repeating the same ones over and over again. When we are afraid to make any error, we may find ourselves stuck in a comfort zone. If we continue to repeat the same error over and over again, it also becomes familiar—a comfort zone in itself. Yet, let's not forget that we can also learn from other peoples' mistakes, sparing ourselves the need to make them ourselves.

But I prefer not to call them 'mistakes', rather opportunities to learn, to adjust our direction and to consider and reflect on our path and intention.

Making a decision requires reflection. When we act with laziness, we choose to stay in a familiar place, in what we know, even if it is not the best thing to do. With time, we become lazy, opting for the easy way even if it may eventually lead to struggle or discomfort. Yet it is familiar, so it becomes who we think we are and is our reality. Is it really a reality, or an illusion we have created and believe in?

We have the possibility to reconsider what we identify with, what we believe in. When we clarify, heal, and access our heart space, (the home of our feelings, gifts and inspirations), we have the chance to nurture that space and reconsider our direction and intention in our daily routine and actions.

We all have a certain Element that is dominant (though, all of them deserve to be taken into consideration). It is not that one is better than the other; they are different and complement each other.

I believe we should walk our path with consciousness, manifesting our visions. But first we must establish, what is our main intention? It is difficult to make any decision if we don't have a clear intention. The intention is our

inner scale. It helps us balance the plus and minus of the different aspects in a specific situation.

Give yourself space for reflection and observe what your main interests are at this time. If your focus is art, what type of art are you interested in? Are you interested in creating art yourself or collecting art from others? If so, are you interested in using the art to beautify your space, to build up a collection, or as an investment or all of the above? Clarifying your vision and intention is a key element in the process of creation.

Our ego can sometimes drive us away from our intention. We may be afraid to lose control or to fail. This will influence our decision. Sometimes, the only way we will find out is by trying, by taking the step. Yet if we fear judgment, a lack of self-esteem can hold us back, making us believe we won't make our goal. Conversely, rushing into things can be another extreme and the flip side of the ego coin.

Leadership can be hard to define. It is interpreted in different ways depending of the context and social group. Let's look at leadership as a skill designed to spur us into action, to motivate us to follow our desires, our motivations and purpose. A leader develops his main gifts and potentials. He is inspired and inspires others to reach for a clear vision.

A leader inspires, brings motivation, guidance and encouragement. His or her actions will be directed, with clarity, towards a vision or goal with a clear intention. A leader uses his or her gifts to support others to use and develop their own gifts.

Are you inspired to be a leader with healthy values, ethics and an honorable cause? The Elements support the development of clear values and skills as a leader.

Using the Elements means that your intention to be a leader will be purposeful, compassionate and loving. Clarifying your intention will be the source inspiration of your actions and visions. I suggest you first practice your skills as a leader for projects that are accessible and meaningful to you, before you try to expand and influence others.

Clarifying a personal vision will be a project that you have close to your heart, accessible to your understanding and one that will expand your possibilities. You will create a clear plan and vision board with your priorities and the steps you will follow. Staying focused on those steps and leading your actions clearly towards your vision is fundamental to develop your skill as a leader.

If you are easily distracted and avert gaze from your personal vision, it will be difficult to lead others towards a bigger vision. Being engaged and committed to your vision will be reflected in your movements, actions, and body language. Your full expression will be aligned with that role that you are undertaking.

Developing people skills comes from the Water Element, (which includes a level of sensibility), as well as the development of your power of influence and emotional intelligence. Yet, it is also in direct relation with all the Elements.

A mindful leader influences his or her environment with clear intention, while honoring healthy values and sensibilities. The discipline and grounding part of the process is fundamental in order to provide a good foundation. This is a key element in manifesting the vision and in making anything happen.

Key Elements for Healthy Self-Esteem

It is important to explore the Fire Element to nurture your self-esteem for without it, you are defeated before you begin.

In some cultures and families, people are taught to be humble and self-effacing, never boasting or bragging about their talents and gifts for fear of looking egocentric. But is the ego really something negative?

I consider that nothing is positive or negative in itself, only in context. In order to fulfill our visions and intentions, we need to have a healthy ego and respect healthy boundaries. This will be reflected by taking the role that allows us to accept our responsibilities, honor our values, and act with compassion, clarity and detachment.

A negative ego is based on judgments, expectations and attachments. A positive ego, on the other hand, encourages a healthy self-esteem, taking into consideration your feelings, honoring your intention and relationships and building up a strong sense of self-confidence.

People who study and apply the yamas in yoga, such as ahimsa (non-violence), asteya (non-stealing), aparigraha (non-greediness), and niyamas (meritorious actions), receive tools to help nurture a healthy sense of self-esteem. For example, ahimsa (non-violence), reminds us to not be violent towards others, but also to not allow violence towards ourselves. It requires care and sensitivity towards ourselves, others and our environment.

A holistic approach to building self-confidence includes the consideration of the Five Elements. It requires commitment towards ourselves and our environment. It can happen only by accepting leadership in our lives.

In the Earth Element, we consider the physical and material level. It reflects how we manage our time, our money, our space and follows a clear discipline. We develop a level of independence. We become more self-confident. Ask yourself, do you respect healthy boundaries?

In the Water Element, we consider our emotions and learn to channel them with intention. We positively influence our environment from a space of compassion. We nurture healthy relationships. In what way do you aim to influence people around you?

In the Fire Element, we build up strength and clear values, to develop a sense of personality, a role for ourselves, using our actions and our leadership to inspire others. We exude confidence and express our feelings with warmth. We are appreciative of our gifts and support others to realize theirs. In what ways do you take leadership?

In the Air Element, we clarify our vision and priorities. We focus our attention towards our vision and intention. Meditation, clarity and reflection are skills that support our evolution and a clear communication with our environment. What is your vision?

In the Ether Element, we are aware that we are here for a higher purpose than just feeding our selfish ego. It is the Element allowing us to stay humble and still have a healthy self-esteem. We allow a space for luck, being alert for synchronicities and for making a leap of faith that is sometimes required to continue our path with harmony and evolution. Are you shining as brightly as you might?

Some initial questions to ask yourself might include:

What are your motivations?

Are your actions aligned with your intention and values?

Are you acting with integrity?

Have you been finding excuses not to act to help realize your inspirations?

Do you take your feelings into consideration when making decisions?

It is a journey of self-discovery, unveiling your gifts and inspirations. If you'd like to clarify some specific aspects and receive support, feel free to contact the DHARMI Institute and one of our holistic consultants and coaches will support you through the process. Together you will explore the key Elements to develop confidence and leadership and set up accessible goals to strengthen your base and confidence.

Considering the Earth Element, you create a clear foundation, organization, program and framework.

Share your inspirations with people who will support you emotionally. Choose to spend time with people who inspire you. Transform fear into excitement using the Element of Water.

Clarify your main traits of character and gifts. The things that triggered certain negative feelings and squelched motivation in the past may not still be impediments today. Explore them using the Element of Fire.

Focus your attention towards uplifting your intentions. Clarify your mind and vision. Release attachment to expectations or beliefs that may hold you back, utilizing the Element of Air.

Realize that people don't care until they know how much you care. Be courageous enough to be vulnerable and show you care. Make a leap of faith. Follow your inspirations with courage, clarity, and intention utilizing the Element of Ether.

I, or one of my team members, can support you to release attachments to a negative ego and to discard old patterns that may inhibit growth and the expression of your gifts. I will guide you through the DHARMI Map to access more of your authentic self, clarify your intention and bring leadership into your life.

Making Decisions Using the Five Elements

Maryanne had to make a fast decision concerning the sale of her apartment in Miami Beach. She was passing through a transition in her life and needed to move on. She received a good offer from a potential buyer very soon after putting the property on the market.

The buyer wanted to receive her answer to his offer within two days and close within a week. Maryanne was confused. She wanted to sell the apartment, but she was going through a career transition and wasn't sure she was ready to accept the offer and move in so short a timeframe.

She came to me to help talk the situation out. We first clarified all the details of the situation. *What was the offer? What was the timeframe? How would accepting it now influence her life and her work? Where she might move and how could it be accomplished now?*

Next we worked on clarifying her intention. *What was it she was looking for at this time of her life? Ease?*

Freedom from financial burdens? An inspiring new beginning?

Once we had established her intention and expectations, we looked at whether accepting the offer and moving would be aligned with a good transition and welcome changes at this time.

Maryanne said that it could be a great opportunity, giving her the money and freedom to do what she really would like to do. The buyer was offering more than her asking price and the money was very tempting. It would give her a good base, economically, to begin a new chapter in her life, though she dreaded finding another place to rent during the time of transition. She needed to employ the Element of Earth.

It was motivating to receive this opportunity, yet she felt some kind of resistance. Emotionally, she felt that it was not comfortable. It was too rushed, too soon to move. She would feel more comfortable first completing the transition in her career and to begin to shift gently after that, making use of the Element of Water.

She was still struggling about what to do, weighing the pros and cons. It appeared as though making such a decision required further alignment in all the Elements— that, by accepting the offer, she might be repressing some important feelings and denying her emotional needs.

The Element of Fire here came into play.

If she were focusing only on linear thinking, it would be fine for her to accept the offer. However, when she opened her mind (employed the Element of Air) to a more holistic perspective, she realized it was not a proper choice at this time of her life.

We took some time to clarify what was her main intention at this time of her life. After a meditation, she answered that harmony and freedom were her main intentions. So we examined all the different Elements from that space of harmony and freedom.

In this review, she noticed that the decision to sell was causing her more pressure and stress than harmony and freedom. We placed that revelation in writing on her Map and I suggested she meditate on it again overnight before making the final decision.

A few weeks later, I saw Maryanne again. She said that she decided not to take the buyer's offer and to honor her feelings and priorities, giving them the value and weight they deserved.

Two months after her work transition was completed, she received another offer on the apartment. The new offer was even higher than the previous one, affording her security and economic support, and even giving her a workable timeline in which to move. She sold her apartment and took her time to complete the transition with harmony and freedom, getting off to a great start on her life's new chapter.

Not everyone will find himself or herself in a situation in which they can optimally experience, express, and make use of all Five Elements. If you find yourself in such a situation, you can still imperfectly apply the principles found within them. You can find balance while filling in for some of your life's empty spaces with meaningful work, satisfying activities and pleasurable hobbies. These will add to your quality of life and bring more balance in your lifestyle.

Mary was in a difficult situation into her marriage. She and her husband experienced much conflict, largely from widely differing opinions. Yet they both believed in strong family values and shared two children. After a few sessions through the Cycle of Evolution, Mary released attachments to some expectations that she had about the way her family should be. Still, she was feeling confused and was looking for hope, inspiration and direction. It was time to clarify her position and make a decision.

In her relationship, though she and her husband shared family values and she felt totally supported on the financial aspect of their lives together, her feelings were often being hurt. Her husband made cutting remarks, was often sarcastic, and they disagreed vehemently on many things, including political issues and how to handle many parts of their lives including the education of their children. She felt as though her intelligence was being mocked and her opinions had little value. She needed to find some balance and nurturing regarding those aspects, in order to keep any equilibrium in her life.

She found a job that was intellectually challenging and where her opinions were solicited and given weight. She began getting together regularly with like-minded people and began sharing more quality time with dear friends. The pressure to get all the attention and nurturing she required from her husband became less intense. Though her decisions created a certain distance from her husband, she made certain to work towards a balanced relationship with him and to respect his opinions, no matter how they differed from hers. They discussed the education of their children and with her hurt feelings no longer presenting such a defensive impediment to the conversation, they were able to compromise on some key points, allowing both of them to get some of what each wanted. She loved her husband and wanted the marriage to continue as long as she was free to share time with friends, pursue her own intellectual development through her work, cultural and social opportunities. Without the added pressures of their earlier relationship, her marriage grew better than it had been in years.

Letting Go of Attachments

Nadia was passing through a time of transition. She was letting go of a dream in which she had invested much energy for more than 6 years. But it was time to surrender her attachment to that dream.

To help her choose a new path, I suggested that she re-center and clarify. Upon reflection, she felt inspired to travel alone, something she had never done. I shared my experience walking the Camino de Santiago (*St. James' Way*) in Spain. She started to ponder the idea.

After thinking it over, Nadia came for another consultation and wanted to clarify her decision.

Her intention was to reconnect with herself and find clarity. When we passed through the process of reflection, we considered where she could go. Which options did she have? A time of research revealed which path was most interesting to her, while also being aligned with her intention. The clearer the idea became, the more motivated she was to act on it. Her enthusiasm and confidence were growing, giving her a good feeling about herself and a burst of energy to move forward into that direction.

We took some time to observe if a walk along the Camino de Santiago was aligned with her emotional values. Nadia was choosing a safe option by choosing this adventure. Pilgrims had walked the path for centuries and it was an adventure that thousands of people undertook every year. Such a trip gave her the opportunity to share her travel with other people along the way if she chose. Also, it was an idea that she could share with her loved ones, without causing them too much worry. It was for the best for her and for her relationships.

When the time came to organize the trip and to find the resources that she needed to make it possible, she had plenty of time and adequate resources needed to arrange for a safe and harmonious journey. To feel even more confident and supported, she chose to reserve the hotel nights, organize transports for her luggage and arrange other details prior to going there.

I was supporting her to develop confidence and enabling her to direct her emotions in a way that was creative and that would keep her on track, rather than scattering her energies every time she was a little anxious. She took a few weeks to prepare herself physically, emotionally, actively and psychologically for the experience and then she took the leap of faith and started on her trip.

Nadia's travel was a very enlightening experience. It moved her emotionally and spiritually and gave her a direct opportunity to shift her perspective towards herself and observe the ways she did things and her approach into her life.

She returned with more confidence and released many expectations and attachments. She could then make decisions that were more aligned with her values as an independent woman.

Surprisingly enough, a few months after she made a leap of faith by reconnecting with herself, the dream from which she detached came into manifestation. That was a response to her total surrender, her openness to accept her path fully.

What would be best to help you clarify and walk a clearer path?

Mindfulness & Stress Management

Air Element: Reflect, clarify your mind, and direct your attention with intention. We experience different levels of stress within our lives. Being mindful of our thoughts, actions, emotions, and lifestyle helps us to deal with stress from a clear point of reference.

Together we first observe the situations, people, and environments that trigger specific levels of stress. Then, using the Map, I guide you in clarifying your perspective and help you understand your response mechanism. Together we explore the thoughts and feelings that have been triggered and discover ways to manage your own reaction in each specific situation. For more information about that specific process, you can read my book of The Cycle of Evolution, which is also based on the Five Elements.

We can change our own perspective, our response and the direction of our thoughts. However, we cannot change others. Change happens through acceptance, forgiveness, compassion and gratitude. When we finally let go of old judgments, preconceptions and emotional attachments, change is possible.

When we consider the Five Elements, we pass through the following steps in order to gain a clear reflection:

Ask yourself where you focus your attention. Gently observe this.

From which perspective do you look at life and at this specific situation?

Is your mindset supporting your inspirations and nurturing your well-being and relationships? Or, do you notice that some thoughts are actually working against you?

The Elements will help clear your mind and help the process of reflection:

Organize your thoughts and priorities into a format that is clear and attainable in your mind (Element of Earth).

Consider if your thoughts are nurturing and commit to healthy values and decisions for yourself, your loved ones, and your environment (Element of Water).

Notice if your thoughts are uplifting and inspiring to yourself and others (Element of Fire).

Clarify your mind and your ideas. Make time for reflection and introspection daily. Take inventory of your current state at this time of your life. Let this inventory not be based solely on outside expectations, but on your personal feelings and observations about your life. Release attachments to old beliefs and preconceptions (Element of Air).

Be open and breathe into stillness. Meditation leads you to a clear space of integrity that is beyond your thoughts. (Element of Ether).

Key Elements for Stress Awareness & Management

Throughout my career in holistic healing, consulting and self-development, I have met many people experiencing varying levels of stress in their lives. In my observations over time, I noticed that everyone had their own personal experience of stress, with individual interpretations and symptoms.

Sometimes we are not even aware of the stress that is affecting us. It becomes so familiar that we repeatedly feed into stressful actions, thoughts, relationships or behaviors. The vicious cycle continues and becomes stronger, eventually affecting our lives by negatively impacting our health, relationships, and overall well-being.

Through the DHARMI Map, I support people and help them explore how different styles of stress relate to the Five Elements.

 Earth Element

In this Element, we consider stress related to the physical body and material aspects of life, as well as basic needs, family, and foundation.

Stress can be caused by environment. This may be through contamination, noise, aggression, chemicals in food or accidents that cause injury.

We can also experience internal stress due to illness, hormonal changes, or dealing with the aging process. We may feed into stress through bad habits, unhealthy diet or a lack of exercise or sleep.

Stress affects our physical health. Becoming aware of your needs and your physical body will support you in nurturing your body and bringing more balance to your life. We can do this by cultivating a sense of acceptance and compassion.

Years ago, I worked with Leyla who was going through a difficult time in her family relationships. She began to lose weight and had no appetite. She started losing hair, and was experiencing high heart palpitations. When she visited her doctor, he told her that her thyroid was not functioning properly. He highly recommended that she begin treatment with medication and possible surgery, as soon as possible. She booked another appointment for the following week to clarify the process. The next day, she came for a private consultation. As I walked her through the Map, she became conscious of a strong sense of guilt about being alive, when several of her loved ones were dying. In the following days, she proceeded with the steps of the Map and meditation, to give space for acceptance, forgiveness and compassion. The inner work that she engaged in was profound, with introspection and discipline to redirect her attention and focus. At the next appointment with her doctor, he was surprised to notice that her thyroid was balanced and functioning normally. There was no need for surgery or medication at that time.

Water Element

Unhealthy relationships can cause emotional stress. You experience stress when you become overly attached in your relationships. This attachment can create a distance from your own emotional balance.

Exploring your relationships includes looking at your family, your relationships with loved ones, work relationships with colleagues, and the relationship with your environment. Your stress affects others, just as others may affect you. Choosing to surround yourself with positive people will help you to find more harmony. Also, developing compassion in your relationships, being sensitive to the community around you and being proactive in offering emotional support to others can help balance your own emotions. By caring for others, you create an enveloping sense of caring. You then surround yourself with caring, loving and compassionate energy that you manifest, fully experience, then care and share with others.

Yet, we also have to consider the relationship with ourselves, with our body, emotions, feelings and path.

Bringing more awareness to your emotions will help you to authentically navigate your relationships. When you accept the shifting of emotions, much like the constant movement of the water, you awaken compassion and forgiveness. This helps you to release attachments, opening the flow within and all around.

There are no positive or negative emotions. It is rather the way we relate, deal, and channel our emotions that can transform them into a positive or negative. Emotions are directly connected to the vital energy. They give us the strength, confidence to express and direct our actions with intention.

Fire Element

You experience stress in this Element when others hurt your feelings or when you allow your feelings to be hurt. Stress also affects you when your self-esteem is low or when the spark of life seems to be flickering. The external pressure builds up and destroys the healthy ego, causing stress when we allow it.

You can also create stress when you underestimate or overestimate yourself, creating an imbalance in your Fire Element. When you procrastinate on moving towards your dreams and inspirations, you put extra weight and pressure on your heart, creating a wound and causing unnecessary stress. Balancing the intensity, the warmth in your expression is a skill that you can learn as you develop that Element.

To heal and nurture your hearts, you must first become aware of your own true feelings and desires, releasing the expectations that you feel from others or that you have towards others or yourself. It takes practice to differentiate between your inner voice and the messages you receive from others. Both are so close to each other that, deep inside, after clearing layers, they can form one. When you are able to do this, you can awaken to your own true calling. Sometimes the reflection and projection can be quite interesting and activate synchronicities in your life.

Some people become addicted to stress. I once worked with a man in Pucon, a village in the southern Andes where I lived for a few years. He experienced a feeling of relaxation after our morning consultation. When I saw him the next day, he said that he had consumed at least three coffees that day, trying to find his normal "stressful" feeling. He didn't believe that he could work or be efficient if he was feeling so relaxed, so calm and clear. Though, at the end of the day, he noticed that he had been very productive. He accomplished many things that day, and completed tasks that he had been procrastinating for weeks. Everything was flowing, with no resistance and no pressure. He could lead his actions with clear direction. It was a very unfamiliar place for him to be.

Air Element

What you see, read, and hear can be a significant source of stress. You may notice that watching the news or a violent film affects your state of mind. Experiencing aggressive language or verbal abuse can also be extremely harmful and traumatic. The pain of this can sometimes be more difficult to heal than a physical wound because the pain is internalized. The internal thought process continues to feed into it. When aggressive and hurtful words come from loved ones or with intense influence, you can begin to believe them. This is one of the main sources of stress.

One morning, Leon was recovering after a long surgery. After a few days, he was feeling good, but then began to watch the news and documentaries about war for the entire day. His energy began to decrease, causing stress within his whole body. After becoming aware of this, the next day he chose to watch a more uplifting television channel, listen to music, and enjoy things that were more harmonious. His healing accelerated and his state of mind noticeably improved.

Your state of mind and state of being will go wherever we choose to direct your attention and energy. Being aware of your thoughts and core beliefs helps to clarify your mind and promote healing. Learning to direct the mind with clarity takes practice and intention. It is similar to training a new muscle and requires constant attention in order to stay alert and effective.

 Ether Element

Fate dictates that certain aspects of life are simply out of our control. We will all grow older as the days pass. We will all die one day, even with the best surgeon, the most cautious driver, the most enlightened guru, or the services of a miracle healer. They are also going to leave this physical form sometime. This physical dimension that we live in is a temporary one.

Yet, there are other aspects of fate that some try to resist. Not all marriages will last forever. The child that you wanted may grow up to be different than you expected. Perhaps you are envious that the talents of your friend are better than your own. It is only through acceptance of your own potential and gifts that you will find happiness, balance, and abundance. A large source of stress comes from resistance to what is—to your own path, purpose and truth.

The gap between your intention, your expression, and your perception creates a stressful reality.

Some people believe that by loving another person, they have the ability to change them to fit their own expectations. Over time, they realize that what they loved was the illusion they built about that individual, rather than the actual person.

We encounter stress when we try to resist fate, or when we believe that we must fully surrender to it with no personal accountability or responsibility. Finding the middle road will support a path to stress management and balance.

Developing the qualities of acceptance, compassion, forgiveness, and gratitude, as well as clarifying your intention, support the process of navigating life's transitions with clarity and strength.

Angela came to see me during a time of indecision regarding her relationship. She felt very stressed over the relationship between her love partner and his ex-wife. It was an aspect in her relationship and life that she didn't have under control. All else was clear and things were going the way she wanted it in her life. Her boyfriend was very compassionate and loving.

Yet, she was very upset for the lack of control she had over his daughter and ex-wife. Angela's stress, frustration and anger were growing more and more intense with time. She wanted to have control. She wanted his ex-wife and daughter to behave a certain way.

Her own resistance and need for control was creating a gap in her life and feelings of dissatisfaction were seeping in. It was affecting her relationship with her love partner. Just the thought of the ex-wife and daughter affected her emotions and caused her stress, intruding on own self-confidence and peace. She was constantly driven away from her center and heart space.

Her stated intention was for harmony, yet she was expressing herself constantly from a very agitated place. Through a few consultations, she began to recognize her own response mechanism, the role she was taking and learned to develop compassion, acceptance and forgiveness. It took a few weeks until she could distance herself from that profound stress that was triggering a direct response mechanism.

Her response came from anger, frustration, fear of loss and a very tight and aggressive form of expression, which was clearly reflected in her body language. Her subconscious thought was, "I am not being heard," which was making her speak louder and breathe less. She couldn't hear anyone around her anymore, so wrapped up was she in trying to have her voice heard by others. That response was causing more distance and tension between her and everyone around her.

The more aware Angela became of her response mechanism, the better she could deal with it and direct her emotions in a way that was more compassionate and stemming from a positive intention.

It was scary to let go of the guards and protection mechanisms for a person with her traits of character; yet, she could gain a little distance and let go of an unhealthy ego. She could direct her expression from a heartful space instead of a compulsive space.

With the time, Angela began to develop more confidence in acting with mindfulness. The stress was becoming less intense and she could manage it with direction and clarity. It gave her strength and brought more serenity in her life. She took time to clarify her expectations and communication. She reflected on the situation, and observed how this relationship was supporting her.

She had strong feelings for the man and his presence was uplifting her sense of love and self-confidence. Her values were respected in her relationship with him. She felt that their values were aligned. He was trustworthy emotionally and also provided her good foundation of emotional, as well as economic, support. They supported each other in the organization and routines of their life, both adding to a healthy lifestyle—one with discipline and a firm foundation. Also, to her, having a masculine figure for her family was important.

The clearer she became, the more she began to acknowledge and appreciate those key aspects that were allowing a quite high level of integrity and connectedness in their relationship and the less she was distracted by outside issues, like his ex-wife.

By focusing the attention towards what really matters, nurturing the core essence and foundation of your intention, distractions begin to dissolve and fade away from your thought patterns, behaviors, attention, and life.

Life's Transition:
Life is a Constant Evolution—Ether Element

Navigate life's transition with compassion, guidance, clarity, and support.

Are you going through a transition in any of the areas of your life?

Truthfully, we pass through constant transitions in our lives. We may experience transitions in our health or our lifestyle. We may experience transitions in our family, in a relationship, in our career, our interests or even the country in which we live. We can deal with some of our transitions with clarity. Others are more challenging to navigate.

When you navigate life's transitions, you can explore them in the context of the Five Elements:

Changes directly related to your health or physical body, or to your family and foundation (Element of Earth).

Transitions that you experience in your relationships (Element of Water).

Changes of inspirations, career, motivations or direction (Element of Fire).

Changes of interest, perspective or cultural changes due to relocation or other reasons (Element of Air).

What if you pass through a big spiritual shift? Opening the door to new possibilities, learning how to deal with all of those awakenings is the purview of the Element of Ether.

Over the years, I have had the opportunity to revisit my perspective in many different aspects of my life. Just as it did to me, the Map can support you when you are assimilating life transitions, searching for clarity and when you are open to receiving the tools to continue your journey within your new reality.

It is also an incredible path to bring your inspirations into manifestation, while considering the Key Elements that lead you to fully experience a new reality, a new way, and a new life.

Loss Ushered in a New Chapter

When Alejandro lost his wife, who passed from cancer a year ago, something unexpected happened. The process of grief granted him detachment from his drug addiction of more than 20 years duration. He actually ceased taking drugs as his wife grew more ill. As she got sicker, he grew stronger. She needed him and he was inspired to take care of her the best he could.

As a business owner, he had always been very successful. He worked hard to fulfill other's expectations, even to the extremes of his being the one to always pacify and enable those around him. Even his employees grew to take advantage of him and he took on more of everyone's responsibilities as time went on.

Alejandro wasn't unaware of his emotional co-dependence. He had always been attracted to people with whom he had to take the role of caretaker. He took the role of caretaker after he himself had gone through a profound trauma and dealt with it by giving even more of himself to others. He followed the steps of The Cycle of Evolution and dealt with the more profound aspects of his co-dependence, yet wasn't yet free of it when his wife got sick.

Alejandro was entering in a new stage of his life. He was letting go of his addictions and co-dependencies. This process gave him a white, clear space to face the unknown. He asked himself questions like, "What can I do if I am free?" and "What is there for me if I stop enabling so many around me and let them live their own lives?"

He worked on clarifying his intention and realized that, though he had always applied his fundamental values towards others, he did not employ them towards himself. He was a good man, the kind who would give anyone the shirt off of his back. His business even had to do with the development of a healthy environment. Yet he neglected himself sorely. He took on so much of other people's responsibilities that he became physically ill and was hospitalized. While there, it became apparent who were his 'fair weather friends', those he could count on only during the good times. Alejandro saw whom he could depend and count upon and those he could not.

He knew that he had finally reached bottom and he was determined to get through the painful experience alone, relying on his own strength and taking back responsibility for his own well-being. He saw the whole episode as opportunity for a rebirth. Alejandro wanted to start with a clean slate and begin from a new starting point. He began concentrating on an intention of caring, for himself and those around him. As he reflected on changing his perspective, he grew more confident and things around him aligned, responding to his new approach, perspective and leadership.

New people, aligned with his values, began to appear on his path. His relationship with those staff members of his who were used to taking advantage of him changed. He began to own his place in the world, to take his own responsibility, honoring his work, business, and energy. His business became more aligned and even more successful. He is now building up a healthy, loving relationship and planning a future with a partner with love and harmony.

Before, Alejandro always had a tendency to put his well-being to the side in favor of others. A constant reminder to nurture the Key Elements for balance and evolution brought him back on to a healthy path. Now that he is more aware and alert. He quickly notices signals in his daily life, which allows him to take leadership with clarity, and direct his actions accordingly. He noticed that he can care for others while being in a healthy space for himself, and that the experience is more nurturing and uplifting for everyone.

When he began to notice his tendency to focalize all his energy in his job, he saw that becoming workaholic was a way to come back into a familiar zone, one of addiction and outside focus. He became aware of this drift in his attention and energy and his new sensitivity to his emotional balance and health called him quickly back to center. This way he could stay within healthy parameters, while expanding professionally and preparing for a new home, which he will move into in the next few months.

Separation and Divorce Lead to a New Career

What to do when suddenly a separation or divorce, with all its attendant complications, happens?

The first step requires a moment of integration, of healing and the need to recenter. The Cycle of Evolution, the other pathway in the Map, supports the first stage in the process. Those first steps support the process to release attachments, detach from expectations and guides you on how to find a new perspective and intention.

Cathy became a mother just before her husband walked out on her. After a time, during which the shock began to wear off, Cathy knew that she needed to see her life from a new perspective and to create new points of reference. Those points of references included a routine and discipline that fit her new reality as a mother, with new schedule adjustments for the child, different food and changes to her lifestyle. Another point was to clarify relationships. Some friends from the past were not on her same level any more, after the separation. Some friends grew distant, while others came closer. Sometimes, when a big shift happens, new friendships are built and such was the case with Cathy. As a married woman, she found some like-minded people that were well in alignment with her family situation. Now, as a separated woman, some judgments or fear appeared in some of her friends who were still in couple relationships.

Cathy's self-esteem also needed rebuilding. Her professional life completely shifted and deserved attention, re-orientation and re-direction. She was even contemplating building a new business on her own, since the separation from her husband also included separating their business relationship. Cathy found herself in a position to rebuild her reputation, her career and her estimation of herself. A new life beckoned.

But Cathy's thought process had to become clearer as she learned to focus on all the new things coming into creation and those yet to come, yet she also had to lean from her new experiences. These aspects are part of the new points of reference she is focusing on, to move forward on her path, with harmony, compassion, strength and confidence.

Clarity in those Key Elements brings a sense of integrity and balance, which created pillars of strength around her. Those pillars are giving her support and a sense of confidence after the loss of former pillar, a point of reference that she had during 15 years of marriage.

All those steps take time to be reconsidered, evaluated, explored and rebuilt. A feeling of victimization can come to the forefront. Cathy has learned to channel this anger and all her emotions, towards creativity, her vision and honoring healthy values during the process of her recovery and reimagining.

Losing Your Job—Gaining Your Integrity

Ralf was informed that he was fired, after working and investing a lot of his energy for 10 years in a big project in a corporation.

He didn't know what to do, But he was clear that he didn't wanted to go back into another similar situation, investing so much time and energy on other people's projects that weren't aligned with his values and interests. He had been feeling miserable at his work, with no opportunity to express his talent or share his values with his co-workers.

He didn't enjoy the projects he was assigned, but the steady paycheck kept him shackled to the job—until he was, surprisingly and suddenly, free.

We first did a few consultations to clarify his mind and release some of the stress that he was still carrying after his job loss. We did so with The Cycle of Evolution.

Ralf was a talented painter and was always interested in the art scene. Once he clarified his intention and vision, we focused on a plan and steps that he could begin finding his bliss in this new direction.

Ralf began saving money to be able to begin an art project of his own. He planned to get a part-time job to make sure he would have enough money to see the project through. Such a part-time job would give him stability, a routine to follow and support (Earth Element).

His love partner was very enthusiastic about his new project. She was providing him emotional support for the new direction he was pursuing (Water Element). It was in alignment with their lifestyle and shared interests. Ralf was very motivated, and he had a boost of energy and inspiration to begin his passionate project (Fire Element).

He began to align his different ideas and options and was having meetings with galleries and other artists to interweave their strengths into a common vision (Air Element). Clearly, this was a good option for him. The Elements were balanced and in alignment, giving him a green light. He proceeded to pursue his artistic passion with joy and inspiration, with a clear positive intention (Ether Element).

Through the development of his project, he and I went through more micro-aspects on how to integrate the Elements in his relationships, in his creative projects, and in the setup of his exhibitions.

Creating a Support System

Joanne, a very caring and sensitive woman, was experiencing a loss in her close family.

We had been working together for some time, with me supporting her on her journey, clarifying her steps using the three pathways on the DHARMI Map. We adapted the directions, depending of her needs and the life situations that happen to her.

One day, as she was spending a few weeks near her mother who was not doing well, she endured a very traumatic experience. She was already aware of the aging process in her mother, who was in her early 90's. Yet that day, her mother didn't recognize her. Staff members at the nursing home tried to explain that Joanne was her daughter, but her mother couldn't remember her.

What was adding to the difficult experience is that Joanne's mother remembered Joanne's sister, but not Joanne. At her consultation that evening, she was devastated, saying to me, "I've lost my mother".

Joanne was in tears for the whole day, but she stayed at her mother's bedside, saying she felt it was her responsibility to be there. She wondered if something she had done or failed to do over the years had brought on the episode of her mother remembering her sister, but not herself. Perhaps she hadn't been a good enough daughter? She felt very lonely and abandoned and had bad dreams that night. The last vestige of attachment to the woman who bore her was taken away from her. She lost her point of reference and had a sensation of floating in the air, profoundly disconnected. It was as if the world was falling away from under her feet.

Joanne tried to cope with this profound sadness and sensation of loss by going away, trying to not feel, making herself numb. She couldn't focus on anything.

To help her deal with the loss, I used the essential oils of the DHARMI-blends of the Elements. We began with the 'Earth Element'. It showed how important it was for her to find a base, a point of support on which to rely, to help her gain her emotional footing and begin to deal with the loss she felt.

The scent was giving her a sense of strength, which she recognized as a good sign. It was a nurturing sensation that flowed into her heart.

I gave her some time and guidance to reenter, and then lead her through the recognition, clarification and setup of the Four Pillars to support that nurturing intention (Element of Ether).

The Earth support recognizes and focuses on the physical and material support that she had in her life. The stability was in having a home, a discipline, food to eat and her basic needs being covered. It was time to for her to acknowledge and be thankful for those things. The gratitude would help her get grounded.

I also drew her attention to the fact that other emotional support was available to her in the guise of two siblings, nephews, and a few close friends around her. She redirected her attention to allow herself to receive that emotional support. (Water Element).

For her confidence, I suggested her to remember some 'sparks', inspirations from her life thus far; the smile of some children that are around her regularly, the events and activities that she enjoys doing and sharing and the love that she has felt warm her heart (Fire Element).

Then we worked on the need to focus her attention and direct her mind towards cultural interests, like-minded people, and cultural activities from which she likes to learn. I asked that she remember that intellectual stimulation moves towards positive attention. Such thoughts were fundamental for her to allow a nurturing space to open in her life (Air Element).

We did a meditation for her to visualize all of this and to nurture her heart space. This brought a sense of healing and more strength for her to use to continue forward (Ether Element).

Honoring Our Feminine Energy

I am sharing with you some key aspects that I have learned as a woman, making use of my feminine energy. I have been working professionally, following my purpose, as visionary, holistic consultant coach, healer, and entrepreneur, on five continents.

I left Switzerland 21 years ago. My plan was not to leave my country, rather to follow a vision and, as the doors continued to open in the labyrinth of life, I continued to follow where they led.

I arrived in Miami a decade ago, where I opened my own company, to share my creation: A unique cultural art form for the betterment of the community in the United States. Included in my vision was passing along my discovery how Key Elements help find balance as we pass through life's transitions.

Let me share my personal perspective on how I used the Map and the Elements to support my integration in a new country, as an independent woman:

Tips for Health (Earth)

A healthy lifestyle is important. I adapt my discipline, exercises and the intensity with which I engage in my activities to correspond to my moon cycle. This has helped me to stay balanced as a woman. I learn about the fruits and vegetables of the season, and feed myself mostly with food that comes from the state or country in which I live. I believe that what my body needs in a specific place comes from the land and climate where I am at that time. The honey that strengthens your immune system in the country where you live is the one that comes from that specific place. It is all about the cycles of the earth, the moon and life.

Nurturing Relationships (Water)

To keep balance emotionally, we need to nurture healthy relationships. This can become quite challenging when we are far away from our family, loved ones or old friends. The new friends will never be like the old friends we've had since childhood. Learning about emotional intelligence is key to relate to the people around us. When you accept what you feel, you learn to relate from a space of compassion, acceptance and harmony. When we change location, work place, position, career, country, culture, we are moved emotionally. This movement gives us the opportunity to release emotional attachments and to relate from a space of flow.

I have always been very sensitive as a woman. Through my life's experiences, I learned to listen to my intuition and to honor if something does or does not feel right. I teach dance therapy for women, helping them awaken their sensual, flexible and powerful feminine energy. Honoring our values and healthy boundaries in our relationships are the keys to staying emotionally balanced.

Motivation (Fire)

What is your motivation? What inspires you?

What uplifts me today is not the same activity, dream or person that did so five years ago. Some are the same, yet in a different way. Perhaps you have noticed this in your own life. Maybe a relationship or experience has consumed your Fire and you are passing through a time of healing. Maybe your Fire feels scattered. Maybe your inner flame is warm and balanced, shining and sharing with inspiration.

Some women are driven by their relationships, others by their career, others towards a clear vision or purpose they pursue, still others by love affairs. Some of us, like me, are inspired by all of the above, while others cannot find inspiration anymore. The Map supports anyone who is seeking to heal, balance, nurture and evolve from any of those points of reference.

Finding hobbies, clarifying my dreams, connecting with people and the community that inspires me, is key to uplifting my energy, staying motivated and directing my energy with a clear intention. I strive to do so every day.

Reflection (Air)

The people in the new country I moved to didn't only speak another language. There was a whole new language in their expressions, in their perspective on life and culture. I received the opportunity to think outside of the box by just stepping off the plane. I had to open my mind if I really wanted to learn from the place and community I had come to live in. I learned to open my mind to a much different approach and new ways of thinking, while honoring my values. When we are mindful we use our potential to select and choose in which direction to lead and direct the process of thoughts, applying the knowledge, experience and wisdom accumulated through time.

A daily reflection and meditation helped me to keep a clear mind and vision and it is a practice I follow to this day.

Intention (Ether)

I think that one of the most important things that allows me to stay balanced through my life and travels has always been my intention and meditation. With my eye ever on my purpose, I can more clearly recognize the synchronicities in my daily life.

Whenever I receive an opportunity or initiate a project, I observe if it is aligned with my intention. If there is a conflict with my values and intention, I recognize that it is taking me away from my path. Learning to follow what nurtures my well-being, and is aligned with my higher purpose, is a potential that you, too, can develop.

I worked with a woman, Jenny, who was very stressed at her work. She was convinced that the type of career that she chose was the cause of so much stress. She thought she had no choice but to struggle and work overly hard, to be successful. Yet her life was just one unending struggle about time, finances and demanding projects. She was at a point where she felt very exhausted and needed a change, though she was not sure in which direction to go.

She noticed that she was becoming more aggressive in her approach to her projects and her business. Though she was very talented and creative, the constant struggle, pressure and stress were draining her daily. Her feminine energy was getting weaker and she couldn't find time or space to care for herself.

Deep inside she had very healthy values and pure intention. Yet, she felt she had to be on the battlefield fighting all day and her response mechanisms were getting more and more defensive.

When we focused on re-centering and redefining her approach to her business, we began by clarifying her values and intention. Her intention was 'expansion and abundance'.

Through the following days she noticed how much she was drifting out of her center and values, trying to fulfill investors' expectations, clients' judgments and expectations. She had learned to give in and direct her power and attention towards their sometimes unspoken (and unrealistic) expectations.

When Jenny began to understand that she could 'create' her reality, she began to complete cycles with her clients and upcoming projects from a new perspective. The new projects that were truly inspiring her and about which she was procrastinating, were becoming more of priority for her. She was creating space for her well-being, and organization, and more time daily to invest in her new project. Though still in a same career, she was driven to try to realize an expanded (and more inspiring) vision for her work.

Jenny found an office space to organize herself and clarify her projects, honoring her values. A natural selection happened around her work.

What Jenny learned was that when we honor our values and stick to our intention, we are not the one choosing with whom we work or don't work. The people around us will choose if they are interested to work under our new conditions or not. When we let go of attachments and expectations, we can focus on creation, based on intention. This vibrational reality that we create will then influence our decisions, conditions and priorities and will attract the proper people and repel those less helpful.

Jenny thought that she couldn't be true to herself and honor her feminine energy in her high-powered type of business. She always had to fight for what she got. Everything had to be struggle. Without difficulty, nothing was valued.

When Jenny began to tune in with her feminine energy she noticed her work was now coming from a space of ease and expansion. Her work was even better and more effective than it was previously when she struggled through every transaction.

Such emotional difficulty and stress will take a toll physically. In the last few years before we began our work together, Jenny had suffered misalignment issues in her hips. It was difficult for her to walk. It had been getting worst and limited her range of movement and hampering her getting around on a daily basis.

When Jenny began aligning her life and giving expression to her creativity, she began literally to 'walk her path'. Soon after we began, she shared that her hips felt much better and she could walk again normally and without pain. After a few months, when her new project was completed and gave her a higher sense of self confidence she noticed a new strength and alignment in her thoracic cage. She could breathe with more ease and stand tall with a positive posture.

By integrating her creative gift in her work and sticking to her values with clarity and intent, Jenny had found her true path that is aligned with her intention and gifts at this time of her life. She was also more motivated, her self-esteem was improving and, thanks to the Air Element, her communication became clearer. She could direct her thoughts and attention with more focus.

It is possible to succeed while being your authentic self, with good values and positive intention, but it does require courage, compassion, clarity, and discipline.

CHAPTER FOUR
Cycle for Creation & Manifestation

In this chapter, we observe how the Elements combine and complement each other to support you in your everyday life. This may be in the way you manage your space and time or in the way you manifest an idea, vision or business.

How can we manifest anything if we lack resources (Earth), or inspiration (Air), or emotional support (Water)? If they really are lacking around us, we may access some of those essential forces within us. We may also be creative and look for them in nature and in our environment, making it possible to access those essential resources.

As we choose to honor healthy values, we are not going to force something that is not yet ready to be, but is instead based on ego, greed or fear. Also, we are not enabling excuses and ego based on resistance, procrastination or patterns that hold us back.

I trust that you are going to use the following tools for a positive intention based on healthy values expressed towards yourself, your loved ones, your community and environment.

The Elements are based on nature's wisdom and I hope this book proves to be an inspiration to apply it in your everyday life with mindfulness.

When we apply this inner ecology and a holistic lifestyle, we directly affect the ecology and environment around us. Changes come from each one of us—the way we act, the way we choose to live, the way we manage our resources and invest our energy. Are we living from a space of greed or allowing balance in our lives?

We can grow, evolve and live in abundance, while honoring healthy boundaries and our environment.

When we bring awareness into our inner ecosystem, in ourselves, and the life we choose to live, this will be reflected in the Five Elements the following ways:

In the Earth Element: We respect and value our space and time, as well as we respect others. We nurture our body with healthy food and a healthy lifestyle. If we care for our well-being and balance our resources, we won't be losing so much energy in over-accumulation. We will also nurture the earth around us and be attentive to health, prioritizing local food from farmers. We will give space and time for our basic needs to be covered in harmony with the environment in which we live. We respond to our needs and recognize our boundaries. We still recognize the need for stability and support to live comfortably and grow. Yet, sometimes, we tend to accumulate so much that we cannot grow anymore. The Earth Element surrounding us becomes dry, covered by so many things that it cannot breathe. Being in touch with that Element reminds us of the basics of hygiene, as well as cooking good food and eating properly and nurturing our bodies. Taking time to nurture those fundamental aspects is like nurturing the roots for our own personal Tree of Life so that it may stay strong and grow healthily.

In the Water Element: We channel and receive the vital energy from our emotions. We allow the flow. After we assimilate and digest, we let go, we detach, in order to release what we do not need anymore. It reminds us to recycle, to compost in our everyday life and nurture our Earth. All the Elements combine and support each other's growth, balance and expression. When we accept to experience our emotions, to feel what we feel and surf those waves of emotion, we are more sensitive and compassionate towards others and our own environment.

Choosing over-processed foods can reflect our choice to over-process emotions. Choosing artificial flavors can reflect a difficulty accepting our nature, instead trying to overdo—forcing situations and outcomes. If instead we choose simple, organic ingredients from the tree in our own backyard, we help bring our relationship into balance with nature and our environment.

In the Fire Element: We become pro-active and more sensitive to our feelings. We take responsibility for our actions, balancing the giving and receiving from a heartful space. We take leadership and genuinely care for the interactions with others and our environment. We learn to not overdo, to stop being busy doing nothing. We balance our Fire and the intensity of our actions. We detach from ego and greed-driven actions. When we love and accept who we are, our authentic self, we also awaken that love and acceptance towards our community and all of nature around us.

In the Air Element: We are freeing our thoughts from contamination caused by judgments, hurtful core beliefs or expectations. We observe our breath and strive for positive and clear visions through a practice of deep respiration, using the very air we breathe as a tool for clarity. When we clarify that sense, we are also more sensitive to the contamination in the air we breathe and the contamination we create with extra noise in our environment (like traffic and other noise pollution) and in our homes. We begin to quiet our own thoughts.

In the Ether Element: It is in this space that we choose to act and live for a higher purpose, one with a pure intention. Considering not only our own well-being, but opening our consciousness to a bigger picture. We encompass those who went before us, those who are with us now, and those who will be coming after us.

When you integrate and balance the Five Elements in your life, business, and relationships, you develop a holistic, integrative way of living that is going to also affect all those around you. Learning to clarify the difference between healthy boundaries and obstacles, limiting beliefs and erroneous facts is fundamental to the process.

It is a subtle line, not straightforward. It moves in constant evolution, adapting to the natural changes that we experience in life.

This line depends of the level of responsibility that we have or that we choose to take on in our lives— whether that is in the material realm, with our families, community or environment.

You can push your boundaries from a positive intention, opening new possibilities for growth, abundance, and expansion.

Others may lack respect and push boundaries from an ego and greed-driven space, caused by past abuse, such as verbal abuse (Air) or bullying (Fire) that wreaks havoc with our physical life (Earth) and our emotions (Water).

Some people would rather stay out of all possibly contentious situations. This is probably not you who are reading this book and striving to balance your life, awakening more consciousness. Despite the others' lack of engagement, they do deserve respect. If you notice that you are in this situation and would like to find support to transcend towards a more engaging position, you can use the tools mentioned in this book or contact the Institute for guidance.

Those working from a positive space will nurture and uplift their energy and that of their community and their environment. Those frightened into inaction or rash reaction may cause harm. It has always been the two forces of yin and yang, light and darkness, and this is somehow part of creation itself.

The Five Elements can be integrated harmoniously for balance within us, and around us and are a way to bring mindfulness into our lives. When we all begin to be more aware of our healthy and negative ego, we clear our mind from contaminations and negative thoughts. We balance our emotions and relationships. We become more selective purifying our emotions and the food we eat. By choosing healthy, balanced food and healthy balanced relationships, we are grounding and nurturing our bodies.

The more we learn to listen to our nature, our senses and our needs (our true inspiration), the more sensitive we are to external contaminations, such as noise and bright lights, that aggressively assail our senses. We notice when some foods are causing harm and choose what feels best for us. Being sensitive to ourselves, mindful in our lives and accepting what we cannot change will directly reflect in our actions and in the environment around us.

Is it really the planet that is in trouble, or also we human beings, who have become more focused on the problems we've created than the solutions? We seem to be driven by external stimulation, told what to worry about (reacting to the shocking stories the media feeds us) and always reacting instead of thoughtfully responding. We forget our innate wisdom and lose our ability to respond accordingly.

Our society encourages discontent. We are bombarded with images of how the 'other half' lives, creating in us a desire for things we didn't even know existed, yet, once seen, we must have. Fine examples are smartphones that had never existed and yet, so soon after their introduction, we can't imagine life without them. A desire was created in us. Some of those are uplifting and supporting our evolution, while others are a built-in discontent. We may lose the ability to stay selective in our choices with clarity and intention.

Being selective doesn't mean denying the facts, but rather choosing our focus, direction and path with responsibility. When our senses are over stimulated, we may lose the feeling of beauty, grace and wisdom, looking for substitutions in food, relationships or material things. When we choose to buy a product, whether it is organic food from a local farmer, processed foods packaged in plastic and sold in a big supermarket, or a big car that contaminates the planet rather than an environmentally friendly hybrid car; our choices feed and empower that object or product upon which we choose to focus.

Likewise, with our time and attention, we can choose either to invest in projects that are humanitarian in scope or projects that are destructive to people and our environment. We can focus on watching television programs and films that are related to wars, rather than focusing our attention towards the documentaries related to healthy solutions. When we are clear about a specific problem we choose to focus on and act upon, we can keep our awareness of nature and mindfulness, directing our own focus towards projects that help to resolve those issues and promote peace and those positive aspects in life.

Taking control of our decisions is a kind of leadership and is not only affecting our own well-being and balance, but also our environment and overall community. Every action, decision, thought and feeling that we nurture in our life, is having an effect in the short-and long-term on our environment and overall community.

When we clarify what we need and are selective of what we will buy, we won't have to throw away so many things that are not serving us. It may serve another person or another purpose. We can direct it somewhere else, with intention. Letting go of such attachments gives us a chance to grow.

The fear of loss and the fear of death may lead many to grasp and attach more firmly or to sabotage. It is a self-defense mechanism that cannot always be managed with discernment. What can we lose? We can lose the beauty of the world, the sharing experiences, living with compassion, and acceptance of the nature and universal law. There is so much we can learn from nature (by observing and receiving), through the experience itself.

Each one of us is one pixel of this fantastic art piece and the world in which we live. It is our responsibility to keep this pixel bright, inspiring, clear and connected.

Through the DHARMI Map, and programs for holistic development, I invite you to develop new perspectives that are aligned with your reality and intention at this time of your life. The object is to awaken new possibilities with compassion and non-judgment, to lead to a clear intention.

Let's observe how we can apply a holistic approach, based on the Five Elements in our everyday life and relationships, and use them to help manifest our visions.

Space and Time Management

Creating some points of reference and a healthy grounding of organization in our time and space is fundamental for our well-being, peace, and growth.

Life is constant chaos, with changes happening continuously in our relationships, in our work, in our environment, as well as in our own needs and desires.

How can we stay centered in such a constantly moving atmosphere?

I have met people so consumed by a relationship that they could not focus on their studies, neglected their friends and even ignored their own values.

Other people are workaholics and forget about their family and their friends in the pursuit of money or to avoid facing problems by practically living at their place of business.

Some were distracted by a hobby and lost connection with their family and their work. How can we find a balance to pursue all of our interests? How can we fit it all into our time and space?

God has given us 24 hours and it is in those hours that we are supposed to balance our life. If we want to do more and what we want cannot fit into the allotted time, we should consider that the additional task is perhaps more than we should undertake, or it can be the time to let go of other aspects that are not anymore nurturing or uplifting to us.

The same happens with how much and what we will eat and drink in order to nurture ourselves and be healthy. Why do we try to exceed those healthy boundaries?

When we focus on a holistic development, we choose to release attachments, limiting core-beliefs and ego-driven actions yet we make sure to stay in a balanced, compassionate and honorable space. In yoga philosophy, these life ethics are clarified through the yamas, and niyamas.

For a healthy lifestyle, it is best to have our space well-organized, with a space to nurture basic needs, a space to share, a space to play and to grow, a space for study and culture, a space to meditate and to center ourselves. If there is enough space in your own apartment or home, you can make sure that each space is set and aligned for each specific purpose.

In Feng Shui, it is shown how much extra space can be unhealthy and cause imbalance. If someone lives in a very big home and use only three rooms out of six, the extra space can be source of stress, distraction and loss of energy—energy that could be used creatively and purposefully.

If the TV is on in the bedroom constantly, this causes stress and won't allow you to receive the rest that you need. The light from the screen, the noise, and the intensity and information overload received through the TV set acts aggressively on your nervous system. Your visual and other senses are over-stimulated. Unconsciously, you open your very personal space to strangers' voices and influences. You sacrifice the space and peace needed to release your daily stresses, to reconnect with your center and to cultivate serenity in your mind, body and spirit. Reading something restful is a much better activity in the period just before sleep. You can also do a few minutes of meditation and journaling to reflect on and assimilate the experiences of the day and to clarify your mind before you go sleep.

We could learn much from children who love to write and draw. Combine this with their curiosity about different surfaces and you understand that they are often inspired to practice their artwork on walls or doors. To avoid always saying "No" to them and risk crushing their spontaneity, a wise parent gives them one wall on which to draw—a wall that is theirs. Just as they learn to expend their creative energy in that dedicated space, we, too, can learn to make use of a dedicated space of our own—somewhere in our home we can write, draw, play or sing music, even dance—giving our creative urges free range to express themselves and help balance our emotional health. Also a dedicated Zen space, put aside for reflection and meditation, gives us a sanctuary away from all the noise, chaos and external stimulation of the world outside, allowing us to turn inward and introduce serenity.

In 1994, I spent some time in India. I arrived in Delhi, with a one-way ticket, eager to explore a new perspective of life and to learn about a new culture and traditions. I found a place to stay at the home of a humble Indian family. They were living on the third and highest floor of a multi-family house. When we needed water, we had to walk to another street with a big plastic bucket to pump some water from the well. It was also a place where many people gathered to wash themselves and their clothes and to brush their teeth. Then we had to walk back with the heavy bucket upstairs. We separated the water, with a part to be used for the kitchen and cooking, and the other part for cleaning.

We used the one big room they had as a living room, a dining room and sleeping space, changing the carpet between each transition.

I was so impressed to see the way they were creating transitions in such a small space. Somehow it was giving a sense of having more rooms, just by switching out the carpet and making use of different scents. It changed the whole atmosphere.

When I was traveling through India, I was also always impressed with how they kept their home clean on the inside, while the street and outdoors was always so dirty. Also, their clothes were dyed vibrant colors. The women had jasmine or other types of flowers in their hair. It was a riot of beautiful colors and scents. I found that country and culture so rich, beautiful and authentic. Yet, I also observed extreme poverty, which made me grateful for what I had and actually enriched the experience and wisdom that I received.

Later on that trip, I had the opportunity to spend some time in a bigger home, with much more space and light. It had one area for the women and another area for the men, where only the males could sit and converse. The women could go in only to serve them or clean the space. Each room was used for specific purposes and was organized with clear intention.

How can you organize your space and time in a holistic, integrative way considering the Five Elements?

Let's begin with your personal space—your home. All the Elements are intertwined. Yet they all deserve dedicated time and attention daily.

First you need what I consider your basic needs space—the main foundation of maintaining your physical self. This includes your main shelter—the bathroom, the sleeping area and the kitchen. This footprint can be improved upon by including a dining area and a space for exercise. This is the Earth Element, your basic space. If you have the chance to include a garden, this will offer more harmony by accessing nature's cycle.

The Water Element requires that you allow space and time for your emotional relationships. In your home, this will include the dining and living area, a space that you share quality time with others. It can also include a den or study where you keep photos, favorite books and anything else that gives you a sense of comfort and nurture.

To utilize the Fire Element, you need a space and time for hobbies, or a place to find inspiration or motivation. This dynamic space is uplifting to you and others around you. You can include music, dance, painting, sewing, pottery or whatever challenges you. You can use this space to help propel yourself out of the comfort zone. One of my teachers said that the biggest danger to evolution is comfort. Many are so comfortable with their Earth and Water Elements that they don't have any spark anymore. Life becomes a routine with family, work and even the same old vacations. I've heard from people who have beautiful families, much prosperity, plenty of leisure time and access to worldwide travel, yet they are bored. They are lacking that spark, that motivation, that energy. Comfort can be beautiful, but it can become empty of feelings and inspirations. Many times, out of fear of loss, people choose to put off chasing any dreams or undertaking new challenges or adventures.

When it comes to the Element of Air, space and time are also needed for reflection and opening the mind to new possibilities. We create a clear set of beliefs about what life is and is meant to be. We may stick to those beliefs so much that the mind can be immobile. We need a space or study and reflection—whether this is a formal library, a secluded garden or just a corner of our kitchen. This will be a space to stimulate the mind with cultural updates, news, documentaries or any form of brain activity that suits you at this time. We need also a space for clarification and integration. This is where we can face the day and its problems and take a moment to breathe, meditate, perhaps pray and await answers which will flow into our consciousness—a place where we sit and are willing to listen.

Ether is the Element that should be present throughout our home as we carry its seeds within us. It is the certain knowledge that we don't have all the answers, but that there is a Divine Energy who is available to help us. We see this energy in all spiritual coincidences, strokes of luck and unpredictable synchronicities. When things just fall into place at the right time, be sure the Element of Ether is involved.

If space isn't properly organized or if the energy is in such disharmony it can even cause physical ailments.

I worked with a family that had two sisters who shared a room, but little else. Their characters were as different as night and day and they didn't get along often. The younger sister developed sleeping problems and back pain. Her attention at school wandered and her grades began to suffer. After consulting with the parents, the girls were separated and each was given her own room. Almost immediately, the younger girl began sleeping through the night. Her back pain left her and her attention (and therefore grades) improved. The girls' relationship also improved remarkably, as they both respected their own space and expression. It gave them space to grow, accept and love each other for who they are.

In a Business Setting, the Five Elements are Also Important

The Earth Element comes into play when you pay attention to the framework and organization of your business. You schedule carefully and make the best use of the resources at hand. You are mindful of the need for security and strict about your accounting methods. You don't hesitate to ask for help and get the support that you need.

The Water Element is used when you employ emotional intelligence in dealings with your employees, colleagues, suppliers and clients. You provide workers and clients a restful place, or just a harmonious atmosphere, where the stresses of the day can be reduced and time can be devoted to bonding between employees and their colleagues or between customers of the business and those who work there.

When you demonstrate leadership in your business and offer motivation to the people who work with you to do their best, you are using the Element of Fire. You expect the best from everyone, challenge them to succeed, alone or on a team, and offer them the space and level of responsibility to develop their gifts. It is an awareness that everyone's feelings should be taken into consideration at all times.

You are making use of the Element of Air when your company encourages time for reflection and brainstorming. You give freedom to the people to let their minds and ideas be expressed and taken into consideration. When it comes to discussion of solutions to challenges the company faces, you are opening the mental doors necessary to find a solution. From such musing, inspiration grows and the communication is clear, lightening the atmosphere.

Ether is the Element that allows you, and everyone who works with or for you, to admit that you can't know the outcome of everything. Ether allows for that Element of luck or synchronicity, the pause that lets some of the unseen, yet very welcome, happy coincidences to take a hand in your company's future. It is where the phrase, "Let Go and Let God" comes into play.

I met a couple who had their own business and were beginning to envision a new project. First they began doing research during their family time, but soon they began to create more time and space for their new project to grow while honoring family time. After one year, they could delegate more of their tasks and business to some people that they trained, allowing them to dedicate two days a week to their new vision that was beginning to take form. They made sure to organize family time and share quality time with their children and as a couple throughout the process. Their time and space management had developed step-by-step, as their vision was unfolding.

Similarly, I met with another family from another country. The wife was interested in following a dream that she had and her husband kept telling her that he would support her unconditionally. However, the day he lost his regular job, they had yet to begin the wife's project.

They had put off pursuit of that dream by saying that, when they had time to really talk the project through, they would begin it. Yet that time never came. But when the husband lost his job and had to reevaluate his life and prospects for future work, the couple revisited the wife's dream project.

Though the priority at this time was for him to find a stable job, as he needed to support the family, the couple decided that they would clear one hour twice a week to focus on developing her own project. This dedicated time and space gave them a chance to clarify their vision, and soon that space began to grow into two hours twice a week. The project became ever clearer and continued to develop, finding its direction and opening the path for manifestation. The wife found she could dedicate more time than just their agreed-upon weekly program and began to setup a clear foundation for the manifestation to occur.

To organize time and space in a holistic way within a company, we take in consideration the main Elements. Each aspect deserves attention in order to allow a harmonious, prosperous development:

Some time and space for clarification of the vision is a dedication to the Air Element, the space for the visionaries of any project. We clarify the intention, the goals and target, to direct the attention clearly through the process of manifestation.

Some time and space for the leaders of the company to motivate others and bring their vision into fruition, is an expression of the Fire. We take in consideration the communication, expression of the identity of the company and members, as well as marketing and image. It is visual and exposed.

The time and space for relationships to allow the bonding of the team is an expression of the flow of the Water. It helps to respect healthy values and to create moments and experiences to share. People like to feel that they are part of something. Such emotional capital is fundamental to any manifestation.

A dedicated time and space within the organization to create the proper framework that respects healthy boundaries, allows for clear accounting and administration is established in the Element of Earth. It is also made for proper creation of licenses and schedules to support the company's work—all of which provide a stable foundation. It requires a common ground and clear points of reference for employees to understand, and for the business to grow prosperous.

Some time and space for integration, for vacation, to surrender and take a step back is fundamental for all processes of evolution. This is when the Ether enters into consideration. This is also the space to give back to good causes, to take in consideration a higher purpose in the realization of your vision.

All those Elements complement each other. Some workers within the company participate in only parts of them, while others are exposed to all the Elements as part of a creating or participating in a company's whole vision. Everyone involved deserves much attention and respect, as they are all part of this greater vision.

When some of those aspects are missing, some energy will leach out and it will be harder for the company vision to be realized. Also, in each aspect of any project, there are other subtle undercurrents that must be addressed in order to allow for full expansion and growth. As long as the first steps are undertaken based on positive intentions, and the company tries to integrate healthy values into an integrative process of development, the company has a chance to become a holistic organization and its projects stand a wonderful chance of growing strong and true and coming into manifestation.

I have met visionaries who didn't want to include the material aspects in their visions, a decision that was inhibiting the full manifestation. They had lovely theories, but they stayed no more than daydreams, without practical application.

I also met people who were working hard to make sure they could live and manifest prosperity, focusing mainly on the Earth Element. But they didn't allow themselves to dream, to imagine and envision something they really would like to see manifest. All their energy was poured into their survival instincts, feeding their relationships and habits. They were running in circles and couldn't see a way out or a path forward allowing them more growth. They had given up their dreams.

In addition, many people like to be part of something bigger than themselves, about which they like to talk and dream. But that is as far as they are willing to go. They don't fully commit and structure their ideas. They stay locked in daydreams and can't concentrate long-term. They can't hold their focus and so never fully dream nor fully give up dreaming and their dream goes unfulfilled.

It is all right to be a dreamer. It can be uplifting and inspiring to follow your dreams. When we choose to risk failure or success, we open the doors to new possibilities.

We also want to be aware of someone's comfort zone. There are two different forms of comfort—when we are trapped in the familiar, a vicious circle or when we make use of our intention to flow in the Cycle of Evolution.

There is the comfort zone into which we enter, when we are in a familiar frame of mind, or enter in a routine. The comfort zone can become a limitation to evolution when we continue in a circle, and we don't take into consideration any new possibilities or options for growth.

There is the comfort zone we are in when we are true to ourselves. This is a moving zone that requires constant evaluation and creativity.

A person I have been working with for some time asked me one day, "Shouldn't we go outside of our comfort zone to grow?"

In this context, he was noticing that he was being pro-active in the direction it felt right to him. He was becoming more selective and detaching from what was not serving him anymore.

New doors were opening on his path with abundance. The process was effortless, yet he was engaged, and committed to his personal and professional development.

Actually, we like to go out of the comfort zone that keeps us turning in circles, to follow the comfort zone that leads us through continuous cycles of evolution.

In this last example going out of his comfort zone would have been to sabotage the flow of manifestation on the current of his life.

Key Elements from Inspiration to Manifestation

Whether it is for business or any other project, we can take in consideration the Five Elements to allow a holistic, harmonious process of manifestation.

This methodology supports the development of your vision with balance and integrity. It is a process that requires a clear intention, vision and purpose as well as the respect of healthy values and strong foundation to find the resources to make it possible.

In this chapter I share with you how the process applies. Yet, for a more clear comprehension and application of the methodology, I highly suggest you to work with a licensed DHARMI mentor or consultant/coach.

We consider the vital elements of your project and intention, including:

Clarifying your vision and reflection (the Air Element).

Identifying your motivations, drive, and mission (the Fire Element).

Considering healthy values and relationships (the Water Element).

Finding the resources, creating a clear structure, and building the foundation for our vision to manifest with abundance and prosperity (the Earth Element).

This Cycle in the Map leads you through simple steps to bring your inspiration into manifestation. You may pass through the steps multiple times in different times of the project development.

When you create a team, you like to have some team members to reflect and focus mainly on one or another aspect. This way everyone can develop his and her main potential, while working together to create a higher vision or purpose.

The main leader, entrepreneur or visionary is the person who takes into consideration the whole process and has the global view to lead the project to completion.

Some people began as artists, involved in their own creations, and found other people to support their projects for exposure and publication. Their attention stayed focused on their main gift, while others supported them using their own gifts. Together they created a shining vision.

Other people have great vision and the gift to see a project develop. They will focus on following the steps on their own. The entrepreneur fills all the roles, being the visionary, the provider, the administrator, the accountant, the networking person, the assistant, the investor and, at some point, even their own first client. Then, as the project begins to grow, they will pass through another cycle and look for the right people to support some of the aspects of their business. With time, they can begin to focus more on their own main gift and potential. They can hire people to develop their potential, which will allow an expansion with harmony and integrity.

Here is a preview of those main aspects integrating the Five Elements in the development of your business or manifestation of your vision:

Intention: You receive an idea or an inspiration. This can come from something you see, someone who gives you a suggestion or a dream you had. It can come from a specific need that you see for yourself, or for the community or the environment around you. In this first step, you clarify your intention, which is reflected by the Element Ether. When you clarify your intention prior to developing or clarifying your idea and goals, your approach to your vision is coming from a place that allows personal development together with the development of your project.

Clarification: You reflect on this idea. It is a time to brainstorm, to reflect on this idea in many ways and from many aspects. It is the opportunity to open your mind to the possibility and creation of a clear vision. When we catch the dream with a clear mind, we bring it into a conscious thought. We process it and perhaps bring it into manifestation. *How open are you to receive new ideas? How developed is your ability to visualize? What are the questions, fears or conclusions that may cause resistance to new ideas?*

In this step you approach and think through your idea or vision from a clear intention that has been determined in the first step. If your intention is openness, then you will open your mind to the new perspective and explore the different options that can unfold from there. If your intention is serenity, give space and time to process the information harmoniously and clearly.

Motivations/Feelings: Is your idea inspiring? Does it motivate you? The Fire Element leads to action. How can the idea be manifested, and what actions should be taken to realize it on the physical level? Be attentive to your motivations. If you feel uninspired or lacking in motivation, there is no need to follow through on the idea. Let it go. If you feel uplifted and a spark of creativity, that is the idea you should possibly pursue. Sometimes we receive great ideas or we are driven by what is fashionable. Or we try to succeed the way others have succeeded. Be mindful that what makes others happy and successful, may not be something that is aligned with your own desires and intention. It doesn't mean that it is better or worse. It is just different.

Intuition/Emotional Values: In this step, you clarify if your intention and vision and motivation are in tune with your emotional values. In the Water Element, we take into consideration how one's personal energy flows in harmony with his or her environment, community and emotional realm. It is a time to consider your 'gut feeling', your enteric nervous system, and what your emotional intelligence is telling you. You will nurture relationships that bond and are in tune with this vision and your intention. This will support the flow and connectedness through the process of creation.

Foundation/Resources: All manifestation requires some resources and a good foundation in order to be able to grow. Sometimes we have to begin small, in order to develop a project with consistency and strength. The development of a clear plan, including establishment of a budget, evaluation of the market and the resources that are accessible, is fundamental for you to pursue your idea. What are the main requirements for it to manifest? Where and how can you develop your project? We all need to have a good Earth and base, a well-prepared garden where to plant the seed if you want it to grow abundantly.

Relationships/Emotional Support: This step consists of nurturing the seed that we are planted so that it will grow with harmony within our society, relationships, family, and environment. You will bond and relate with people who are aligned, sensitive and supportive to your intention, values and project. You will be sensitive to the environment and the community in your process of development.

Goals/Confidence/Leadership: In this aspect, we approach the Fire Element from a different angle. As you already have a clear intention, vision, values and plan, it is time to set goals that are challenging and inspiring. What are your goals? You can set goals that can follow step-by-step, helping you grow with confidence. The creation of capital comprised of courage and confidence, requires attention to your feelings. You need a sense of leadership in uplifting your Fire without consuming you or others around you. Building up the Fire takes time, dedication, and determination. This is the expression of the identity and image of your creation.

Communication/Directed Expression: This step requires a high level of focus in your direction, target and vision. You will communicate your project and vision with credibility, integrity and clarity. It is only when you truly believe in your intention and vision, that you can communicate it clearly with the right people at the right time. The more convinced you are, the more influence you can have with others.

Surrender: When you enter into this step, it requires a "leap of faith". When you have completed a first cycle of visualization and evaluation with clarity in all Five Elements, you can enter into the next step with confidence, direction and determination.

You will then pass through another cycle, being actively engaged in the process of manifestation. You will make it happen, using your leadership skills, honoring your intention and respecting each step in the process.

I worked with Iris, who was feeling stuck in her career and self-development. She was developing new ideas and her job was not giving her a sense of fulfillment anymore. Some projects that she had worked on were challenging, interesting and exciting in the past. However, at this time, she was becoming frustrated. This was affecting her relationships and her self-confidence. The stressful situations were taking her away from following a healthy discipline. She was growing and needed to find a way to restructure her business, so as to be able to continue to grow with harmony and inspiration using her gifts.

Iris looked successful, yet her business was filled with struggle, stress and allowed no time to take care of herself and her well-being. With all the hours she devoted to her job, she wasn't seeing enough return financially and in her quality of life.

She and I passed through the Cycle of Evolution to clarify the source of her stress, see a clear intention and determine the new direction her business should take.

She couldn't continue to scatter her energies. She already had a very good professional reputation and was well-known in her profession, but needed a shift into more harmonious, abundant and integrative ways to use her talents.

She wrapped up her old client projects and began to focus on a more structured business aimed towards bigger long-term projects. Those were going to offer her more time to use her creative skills, more space and freedom and more prosperity. They were also a bigger responsibility, yet the compensation was more aligned with her values.

She also decided to initiate another idea and plan—the restoration of homes. It was time to develop the concept and make it happen. On the way, she met many obstacles that required flexibility, compassion and consideration. Yet, she made sure to stay true to her values and intention.

She found a house and investors to support her project. But the two investors brought to the project entirely different value systems. One wanted to play it safe and go slowly developing the project step-by-step. The other was in a hurry and wanted to control all aspects of the project, stifling Iris' creativity.

She began to feel a sense of insecurity conflict and constraint. The foundation wasn't clear and lawyers needed to be consulted to clarify all parties' roles and responsibilities for the project. Instead of plunging headlong as she might have in the past, she shifted her behavior and allowed the time required to clear the base and her own emotional values. Through this choice to stay in her truth, the investor in a hurry pulled out of the project.

Natural selection happened. Iris was then free to pursue her vision and honor her values. Surprisingly enough, she began to receive unconditional support from other sources. These gave her the opportunity to use her gift creatively and follow her vision with abundance and clarity.

Below is the way I supported Jose in incorporating vision considering the Five Elements into a project.

Jose had an inspiration. His idea came from feeling a lack of a way to healthily nourish his body in his busy life. He was always looking for healthy meals at accessible prices that he could grab on the go. As he couldn't find them, he thought about developing that concept and business himself.

He first was inspired to create a healthy fast food business. But he noticed very soon that he didn't have the resources to make that happen, nor would he unless he could convince a team of investors to give him working capital.

He took some time for a clear reflection considering his motivations and his vision in the short and long term, but it was so far from his reality at that time and the resources that were accessible to him.

He noticed that some aspects were not in sync. He could visualize clear goals, but noticed that they were not aligned with his values and very far from being able to be realized with his current resources.

So I suggested that he first clarify his intention.

He hadn't thought about an intention. His idea and motivation was driving him outward, away from his own center. This gap could cause a certain level of stress through the whole process of creation.

After some introspection, his intention became clear. He needed balance.

He wanted to have a more balanced life and that was inspiring him to eat healthier, while still working and sharing quality time with his family.

His first understanding and idea was to create the project in order to find balance. I suggested to him to create the project from a balanced perspective, step-by-step, as much as possible.

When he began to think about his vision and project from a balanced space, he noticed that he could begin the project with some of his own investment, by creating healthy protein bars, with raw and GMO-free ingredients. He had a friend who had a location and knew people who could begin to develop the project with him. This wouldn't add more stress in his life. It would reflect balance and help develop the healthy lifestyle he wished to live.

He was motivated to set some short and long-term goals that would give space and time for the business to grow organically, the same organic process he wanted to use with his foods.

He was clear that his main goal right now was not to make a lot of money, rather to experience balance along the journey and share it to support others.

In the next few months, he created a good foundation for his vision and began to produce and sell his products to people around him. Soon enough, people began to share with others and the business began to grow.

He noticed that he was becoming overwhelmed after a few months and was getting away from his intention of 'balance'. It was time to restructure, to delegate, to expand his business to the next step. He wanted to make sure that he could guarantee the healthy and excellent quality of his products. So he chose to surround himself with people who were also looking for high quality food and services.

Natural selection happened around him when he began to clarify his requirements and conditions. Those who were not sensitive to his intention and ethics went in their own directions. Instead of beginning his journey with a big loan and weight on his shoulders, he chose to invest the little he had, and then, as his company was growing, he could invest more. His business expanded harmoniously. It gave him the space and time to stay true to his values, provide quality products, and to learn about this new business with clarity. He could grow, while experiencing balance with his family time, work, and vision manifestation.

His commitment was honored and shared with others around him, and his team was motivated to follow in that clear direction.

Part of My Story

I arrived in Miami after living for 10 years in different countries, traveling and teaching. I had been on the road, following a path off of the social grid for a long time. I was moving too fast from place to place to settle and anchor myself properly in any of those countries. From Europe to Asia to Australia, through South and Central America, it had been a journey with me traveling continuously. I always could share, heal, study and support people on the way who valued my services and knowledge. This is how I supported myself and continued to realize my mission.

After so many years of research, exploration and study, it was time for me to reenter society. Switzerland would have been the easiest choice for me. However, with the suggestion from a shaman from Chile and one from Holland, I considered the option to come to Miami. North America had always been the last place on my list of where I wanted to visit or live. Yet, it was a time for me to face that resistance and let it go.

I arrived in Florida, knowing (and then only slightly) only three people: two from Brazil and one from New England. Though they were very busy with their own obligations, they gave me support, helped me with a few contacts, found a place I could rent for very little cost, and shared what was most valuable of all—their friendship.

My main intention in settling in Florida was to assist people in awakening and to help add quality to their lives. I was here to support the community.

After I clarified the process and my intention, I opened my own company with the little savings that I had from my work. I wanted to bring a unique cultural art form for the betterment of the community in America and began my DHARMI programs here.

At the beginning, I made some valuable connections. I worked together with other people, joining our strengths and exploring the forms to build up a project. After a few years, we noticed that we had similar visions, but that our paths were diverging. I learned a lot through this experience and found more clarity on the direction I wanted to go at that time. I needed some time to settle and ground myself into this new reality and strengthen my base before moving on too quickly.

I noticed that I had to stand my ground, stay true to my intention and honor my own rhythm. We all have a different rhythm and ways. It doesn't mean that one is better than the other. Our paths meet for a reason. We can learn, grow and evolve together. Sometimes the paths continue together, complementing each other closely for a long time. Other times, it is for shorter periods.

In the following years, I prioritized some aspects in my life to which I had to reconnect. I needed time to enjoy my friends and family and to learn new skills in this new place. I needed to nurture my base and strengthen my foundation to have more stable ground to step on. When that aspect became more harmonious, strong and fulfilled, I could reconnect with the initial vision of my arrival and concentrate even more on perfecting my DHARMI programs.

All has begun to take form with clarity. The vision has become clearer. I have the resources accessible to make things happen. I am more stable and have a point of reference that is strong enough to give me confidence to follow on my own path and direction. The more I stay true to my gift and my intention, the more clearly I can organize my time, my resources (Earth), relate with healthy values through the process of creation (Water), lead and direct my actions honoring my own rhythm and feelings (Fire), as well as clarify my vision and the way to communicate the teachings with clarity (Air).

While staying in my intention, I am noticing that it is all expanding with clarity, motivation and compassion. This gives me space for new possibilities.

I am now the Founder and President of the DHARMI Institute, headquartered in Miami, providing my services in person and online. Some licensed facilitators and holistic consultants/coaches are now offering their services, using the DHARMI Map in Australia, Israel, Switzerland, Texas and Florida. I am now initiating another Institute in Montreux, Switzerland.

From a clear intention, the vision began to grow and expand worldwide, even though I am based in one place. I still continue to travel and I am looking forward to seeing where my intention and path will be leading me next.

Completion of Cycles and Liberation

Sometimes when we feel uncomfortable, we may rush away from a relationship, from a job, from a situation that is triggering emotions that are unpleasant, or that we don't want to deal with anymore. Is it that we don't want to deal with the job situation or with what is happening around us? Or is it that we don't want to deal with the emotion or judgment or reaction it triggers in us?

Of course it is best to focus our attention towards positive, nurturing relationships, though we may have to deal, at certain times, with uncomfortable sensations in order to grow and have a clear shift.

There is a fine line between running away and healthily completing a cycle, or pushing further into something that is hurting or unhealthy for us.

We all experience stress at some time in our lives—whether emotional, professional, psychological or physical stress. This stress is often the reflection of a gap between our inner rhythm, or true self, and our outer experience or actions.

We may perceive that the stress is coming from things outside ourselves—work, family, and our environment, when in fact those situations and circumstances are the secondary causes of our stress. They trigger a reaction within us, yet they are not the root of the stress, the stress itself is in our response and reaction to these external factors.

If we try to change our outer circumstances and choose to move to another location, or to change partners, or look for another job, we will experience a temporary release — until the same reaction within us is inevitably triggered again by our new set of circumstances and unless we complete cycles mindfully and move on with intention and clarity.

When we deepen our understanding and self-awareness, we can access the primary cause of our stress, which is our response mechanism reflected by a core belief paired with a reaction.

Through the DHARMI Map, we are able to access the primary cause of our stress, allowing transcendence and liberation from a lack of something we think we need or a pain memory. This cycle is reactive and feeds back on itself. Our intention is to awaken compassion, gratitude and acceptance—to transcend into a space of clarity and integrity.

The primary cause of stress is that part of yourself to which you have created attachment—which is your ego. We may have developed the ego consciously or subconsciously through accumulated past experiences. This small self may come from past memories or may even be the product of an inherited condition. When we awaken compassion, acceptance and gratitude, we can transcend to connect with our more expanded Self. We then can access a healthy, conscious way of being in direct connection with our heart center. We can then access a healthy and mindful way of being.

When we train ourselves to align with this new space and point of reference, we empower our Vortex of Energy, align our frequency and relate to the secondary causes of stress with more ease and awareness. Our new vibration and realization invites expanded possibilities with grace and abundance.

Completion of a Cycle in a Relationship or Separation

Sometimes when I work with people who are passing through a difficult time in their relationship, they discover that they actually have to divorce a belief. They may have an impulsive reaction to a trauma, preventing them from allowing a new cycle in their relationship. If they open to such a cycle, they invite more compassion.

Sometimes, when people get closer to their own heart center and true self in the moment, they can drift apart from their partner. In other cases, it brings both people closer to each other. We are always three in a relationship: you, your partner, and the spirit of love. When a relationship is based on ego, fear, or attachment, there is no space for love.

As a child, I experienced the separation and divorce of my parents and the new marriages that they built afterwards. I suddenly had half-brothers, a stepbrother, stepmother, stepfather, and so on. I had a lot of healing to do, in my early adulthood, from the traumas and confusion that I experienced at an early age. I began to seek the path—my own path, my own inner voice and guidance.

It takes courage and faith to follow our heart and nurture healthy relationships. Many people who pass through divorce or separation must contend with feelings of stress, depression, anger, fear or emptiness. Many feel lost, not knowing how to manage their change of status, their life, and new perspective. The sessions and guidance through the Map allow them to re-center, rebuild confidence and clarify a new perspective aligned with their new reality.

We can take in consideration the Five Elements to complete a cycle, instead of causing an unnecessary trauma. It doesn't mean that it won't be painful. Yet, it will be mindful and based on a positive intention.

Sarah was feeling depressed in her relationship and family. She had all that she thought would bring her happiness: a handsome husband, a nice house, two children, her own car and plenty of time and abundance for shopping and to take care of herself. She and her family also traveled regularly to visit relatives and go on vacations to beautiful places. Nonetheless, she was feeling depressed and unfulfilled and was blaming it mainly on her husband.

They had more conflicts and the children were beginning to notice and hear their fights, which they couldn't hide from them.

Sarah wanted to just cut and go, to set herself free.

Yet, during her DHARMI consultation, Sarah noticed feeling the same unpleasant emotions about other people and situations, not just about her husband. Through reflection, she began to recognize that she had a feeling of emptiness, insecurity and depression even before she was married.

Sarah could run away from her husband, but it wouldn't mean that she wouldn't feel depressed anymore. What she learned first was to accept her emotions. She became more aware of her defense mechanisms and responses. After some reflection, she noticed that she felt vulnerable and powerless in her love relationship. In order to be loved, she believed you had to give up yourself. She was giving up her ideals and values, neglecting to nurture her self-confidence. She began to trust others more than herself. Her own Fire had become weaker as the years passed.

Following the Map, we began to explore a way to integrate more of her feelings and desires into her life. In the following weeks, she began to take more leadership and express her wishes. She began to build up more confidence in suggesting options for places she liked to go, things she liked to do, and found some time to pursue hobbies which she had not allowed herself before.

This process awakened some fears and insecurities in her. Deep inside, she thought that she couldn't be herself while being in a relationship. Her priority was always focused on her husband's and children's needs, trying to hold the family together, trying to please everyone. Sarah became aware of a fear and trauma of separation that she had experienced in her early childhood. So she kept holding on to that in her own family now, putting herself aside. She began to feel resentment and was expecting that the others would read her mind to fulfill her desires and meet her needs.

She first thought that the only way to find herself and do things that she was interested in, was to separate or divorce. She thought that she would have to fight and that it would be a very hard process.

As she began to take leadership and express her Fire, she was surprised to notice that her husband and family were completely supportive. They were pleased to see her growth.

As she was completing a Cycle and directing her attention to flow with leadership, she had awakened more ability to care for the others around her. Life and her relationships became lighter and more fulfilling.

When we examine preconception, we may find we needn't separate ourselves from those we love, but can gain the space to develop our own well-being, freeing us to evolve.

Paths Sometimes Diverge

Through the process of separation or divorce, there are many aspects to take into consideration about what you keep and what to let go. Yet it is key to find a healthy way to navigate those transitions. You must learn to honor your values and respect your priorities while opening a space for more clarity, compassion and objectivity.

The steps in the Map support the release of attachments, stress, and anxiety, while healing trauma stored in the pain body and reconnecting it to the heart.

A separation often brings a state of grieving— for an illusion, a dream, a belief, or a conflict. Many people lose their center and values through relationship difficulties and separations. When we find a way to empower the connection to our heart, it is possible to build a healthy, balanced relationship with ourselves and discover a new level of confidence in relationships with others.

Here are a few first tips on how the Map and cycle through the Five Elements can bring support in a process of separation:

In the Air Element, you will take in consideration your own belief and judgments about your situation and transition. Some people think that they lost "everything". Others would think that they failed, while someone may feel themselves finally free. A moment of reflection to observe your own perspective towards your situation will help you contemplate your process of thoughts.

Then, you can observe how your feelings are affected, how those thoughts affect you and your way of dealing with the situation. You'll see as well as how this situation affects your confidence, your actions and decisions. This is when the Fire Element comes into consideration.

Deepening your awareness, you will bring your attention towards your emotions, and see how you channel the emotions that you experience at this time. Take into consideration your emotions and observe if you get too attached to your initial feelings of sadness, anger or grief. You may resist the flow that could lead you to release and find more compassion. That is when you channel the Water Element.

In the Earth Element, we consider how you respond physically. Some people cannot eat, and stop their personal discipline. Others would do physical exercise to release the emotional stress. *Is there a specific area in your body where you store the emotions, stress or pain?*

Being aware of all those aspects will give you more clarity about your point of reference. If you can accept, forgive and surrender to what is, to your own form of experience and response, you can then find a clear intention. The intention can be strength, love, clarity or any other that gives you a sense of nurturing, centeredness and that inspires you to focus. This will be the seed from which you can grow. You will be supported as you deal with the situation from an intentional space, and have tools to manage the emotions and responses that the situation triggers within you.

When we are mindful of our present, we can open new doors and lead our way with clarity. As mentioned in a prior example, you can then restructure a new life passing through the Elements in a creative way.

Completion of a Cycle at Work

Gil was becoming more frustrated and stressed at his workplace. He wanted to do something different. He wanted to have more free time. He was seeing people who were successful around him being independent. He was seeing them being freer because they didn't have to deal with the same pressure or obligations that he had. They were their own bosses.

He was not aware of the other levels of stress, discipline and responsibilities that it required to have your own business.

He began to explore the different possibilities around him and entered into the The Cycle Through the Elements, passing through the Elements for creation as mentioned earlier. He chose to begin another activity on the side of his daily work.

He kept his day job, but as he was beginning to feel more confident about his new part-time venture, he noticed he wasn't sure he was ready to leave it entirely. It was challenging for him to just pack and go. He became more aware that he was working there not only for the money itself, but for the stability, security and sense of pride and the acknowledgments that he received.

Now that Gil's new career was helping him build more self-confidence and presenting him more opportunities, he noticed a reduction of stress and frustration at his day job.

During his process of self-development, he began to have some responsibilities at his day-job. He enjoyed using his gifts and having the opportunity to develop his potential in both his activities.

He was not ready to leave his day job. His perspective had changed in the last few months.

With reflection, he clarified what were his priorities and main motivations. He still wanted to stay involved at his workplace, with the team that he began building using his new sense of leadership. But he couldn't continue giving so much of his time and space to this job.

He prepared a plan for a more efficient schedule and more responsibility based from his own remote workplace. He arrived at this plan by considering the Five Elements.

He compiled the ideas using the Element of Air.

He pointed out his leadership skills and ability to motivate others using the Element of Fire.

He took into consideration the long-term relationship he had established with the company, as well as the one he had created with his team, using the Water Element.

He suggested a three-month probationary period, where he could continue to be productive and fulfill his responsibility, starting from his suggested common ground, utilizing the Element of Earth.

He was completing another cycle at his workplace. He had more freedom, while still supporting the vision of the company he had been working for a decade. After six months, he was noticing a well-balanced quality of life, while nurturing his own project, and still holding on to a stable job, which gave his family security.

Completing a cycle is not always closing a door.

It can be opening new doors, releasing some patterns and ways that are not working for you to navigate towards a space that is more aligned with your inspirations, values and intention.

CHAPTER FIVE
Key Elements for Communication

Communication is the bridge that enables you to relate to others. If you choose to reach out to someone, you need to communicate. If someone wants to reach you, they have to communicate.

Just a word can bring support, can inspire, can hurt, can uplift and can bring comfort. Whether expressed or not, a single word can have a major impact on our lives and the lives of others. That is when we notice the power of a single thought.

These days, communication is happening at high speed. We receive infinite information every day through the internet, satellite news, TV, radio, social media, letters and the people around us. Communication also happens through words, touch, images, smells, tastes, sounds, 'vibes' and even through silence. How can we find clarity amidst all this information coming into our lives?

Some people will be driven by external information, which could cause attachments and lengthen the distance from their inner peace. Others will try to find balance, giving themselves time and space for reflection and integration.

The more we know, the more we notice that we don't know. In some aspects knowledge can support wisdom and evolution. Sometimes an accumulation of knowledge can create stress, more doubts, and hold back the development from a wise perspective, and clear intention.

What is reality and what is illusion? What is true here and now may not be true then and there. We are free to think what we will. We all have a different perspective, perception and expectations.

When we awaken consciousness, we enter into a space of clarity, compassion and respect in our communications.

Our awareness is expanding every day, bringing news about what is happening worldwide. And yet we often have no space left to awaken an inner awareness and consciousness in our relationships. Sometimes we can find a gap between the inner awareness and the external matters. The Elements when used for communication gives you tools to create the bridge between yourself, and your surroundings.

The overwhelming flow of information can build a resistance. We can become reactive, responsive and lose our ability to respond and bring clarity to our communication.

How can it affect others and ourselves, if we take the time to clarify our intention and thoughts before sending a text message or engaging a conversation?

As we rush through our lives, we can become impatient and get used to instant gratification. We may develop a response mechanism, going on autopilot, losing the sensibility, attentiveness and consideration of healthy values. We may not be clear about the message we like to communicate or share. We may feel an urgency to react, not respond. Yet, a thoughtless expression can mislead us and the other party who is involved in the communication.

Is it best to act right away or the right way? Maybe it can be the right way, right away. There are many forms and ways to express ourselves, to share and relate with our environment. When we consider the Five Elements in our communication, they ask us to pause, to relate with clarity and intention.

How do we integrate the Five Elements in our communication, as well as our personal and business relationships?

The Air reflects the psychological aspect and the clarification. *How do your core beliefs and expectations affect your comprehension, reflection and attention?*

The Fire reflects our self-esteem and leadership in your intercommunication. *Do you interact with warmth and uplifting energy?*

The Water reflects our emotional intelligence and the way we channel our emotions. *Can you channel your emotions with harmony and compassion in your relationships?*

The Earth reflects the support and foundation. *Do you have a good discipline and respect healthy boundaries?*

Honoring a positive intention, being alert to life's synchronicities, staying centered, and detaching from expectations is considered in the Element Ether. *Are you allowing space for everyone's uniqueness and authenticity to unfold?*

The Five Fundamental Elements combine to allow integrity in our communication. The process aims to integrate new levels of awareness and mindfulness in our relationships.

We are all interconnected. It is inspiring to observe nature's wisdom, in the way in which all is intertwined, related and connected with each other. Sometimes it can appear very chaotic, yet it is perfectly aligned. It is in constant movement through different dynamisms, rhythms, and cycles.

As human beings, we tend to hold onto patterns and outdated expectations. We may freeze and try to stick to known patterns, resisting those natural movements and changes in our interactions, needs, and priorities.

We learn one way and try to stay with a safe solution, though the solution that works best in a given situation may not be as efficient another time. Holding onto only one way can limit the natural flow and growth that occurs in our lives.

The more tools and life experiences we have in our hands, the clearer will be our communication and adaptability in many different circumstances.

When we try to hold onto things outside ourselves, this attachment, and the expectations it creates, limits our evolution and the evolution of others around us.

It is when we accept and surrender that we can take leadership and control of our lives— clearing interactions and allowing the flow of manifestation.

When we attach or fear change, we can create co-dependence, and lose track of our own path and intention. It is as if we have anchored our boat somewhere and stopped following the flow of the river. Day-by-day the gap and resistance gets stronger and stronger, causing stress and frustration.

We live in a time when people are becoming more mindful and being more attentive to nature within and around them. It is a blessing to see how many people, organizations and communities are now becoming more sensitive to the environment and more attentive of the need for a healthy, balanced lifestyle. It is cool to be kind. It is laudable to bring mindfulness into our conversations and lifestyle. It is inspiring to support a higher purpose and good cause for the betterment of our community and environment.

How do we reflect the Elements in our communication?

In some circumstances, we may need to make use of the Earth Element and be very assertive and grounded. That is when we will use a solid and supported body posture and form of expression. Our tone of voice is contained, giving a sense of security and support.

When we enter into an emotional experience, or when we consider that it is time to bring a sensitive, emotional, and nurturing aspect to a relationship, we deal with the Element of Water. Our expression flows, taking into consideration emotional intelligence, observing how we feel, and listening to our intuition.

When there is a lack of motivation, it is the time to uplift the dynamic, by engaging with the Element of Fire and seeking inspiration. This is when you take leadership and become proactive. Being sensitive to your feelings and the feelings of others is bringing warmth to your relationships.

When you notice doubt, clarification from the Air Element is required. It is when you ask questions, clarify your communication and allow a space for clear reflection. It brings lightness and clear understanding, allowing you to open your mind to new ideas and truly express yourself and your true meaning.

Ether is a space for surrender and alertness to the synchronicities that appear on your path. It is the pause that gives space for integration. Things may not be in our control, yet they are in the control of the Universe. Making use of Ether allows us to bow to that spiritual control and be fully present.

Each Element can be expressed with a clear tone of voice, from your choice of expression, body posture, and rhythm in the interaction, all of which should be aligned with your intention.

I integrate the following aspects to support a holistic, integrative communication based on the Five Elements:

 Presence, awareness (Ether)

 Reflection, mindfulness (Air)

 Leadership, body language (Fire)

 Emotional Intelligence, emotional support, positive attention, caring (Water)

 Manifestation, support (Earth)

Presence-Awareness

When we are present and awake, we can relate and communicate with clarity. It requires meditation, focus, alertness and clarification to access a space of stillness and attune to an intention.

Do you communicate in a way that is based on a reaction to past experiences? This can influence your current relationships and communication.

What do you intend to communicate and to share?

You may choose to be involved in a relationship, with the expectation that the other person will change, conforming to an illusion or fantasy you have, instead of accepting and loving that person for who he or she is.

If you have been hurt and carry some resentment, you may respond from a defensive position—even when people approach you with kindness and positive intent. If you have felt humiliated in the past, you may go out of your way to look for acceptance, holding back your truth and real potential.

If you have been successful and received lots of attention, you may relate from a space of power and self-confidence. When you are fully present, you can communicate from a noble place, with clarity.

Here are a few ways to bring your awareness into the present moment, into the here and now:

Observe what surrounds you (external). Notice where you are. *Who is involved in the situation? What is happening? What is the context? Is there any specific smell, music, or lights that catch your attention?*

Observe your inner state of being. *What does this situation trigger in you? What is your behavior and role in the situation? How is your breathing? What is your intention? Is there a smell or anything that triggers memories (your innate emotional intelligence) and specific reactions in you?*

When you are fully present in a situation, you can recognize your location, like a personal GPS, which allows you to establish a point of reference to communicate with clarity and openness.

When you are present, you are attentive and alert. You can choose to focus on a clear intention and be free of expectations towards yourself and others.

When you release attachments, you allow a pure state of Presence. You can tune into the vibration of the moment and communicate appropriately. The more you clear layers of attachments, traumas and expectations, the closer you get to your heart center and a space of stillness.

When you meditate regularly, you develop your potential of concentration and focus. You become more alert and open to explore life's wonders without preconceptions. Beginning and completing your days with a moment of reflection and contemplation gives you the opportunity to clarify your mind and access balance. You become more attentive to the synchronicities on your path when you are alert, centered and present.

Intuition awakens when we connect to each other from a pure and clear space, not only listening to words, but also to the space between words—body language and vibration. Our intuition is very influenced by our own past experiences, beliefs and interpretations. It requires practice to develop the quality of 'Presence'.

During her training as DHARMI Holistic Consultant, Renata had homework to complete, integrating the Elements in her communication with three people. The best way to integrate a theme is by applying it in one's own life. She didn't know with whom she could apply it outside of her family and I suggested to her to begin with being present.

She understood that it meant that she had to release expectations and stress. She had to center herself with her intention through meditation.

The next day, as she was teaching a yoga class, one of her students had a strong reaction in the middle of the class. Renata approached her and suggested she honor her body, her state of being, and respect her limits at the time. First Renata was feeling reactive, yet she remembered to practice 'presence'. She chose to stay in her center and continue to lead her class with harmony, while caring for the person who needed more particular attention. Then the flow could continue with harmony.

After the class, she took a few minutes to speak with the student in question. She began by being in a space of equanimity and in tune with her positive intention. From that space, her student felt her support and Renata could lead a conversation integrating all the Elements through their communication.

Reflection-Mindfulness

In the Element of Air, I take into consideration the clarification in the thought process and reflection in conscious communication. When you listen attentively, you will hear what the person expresses and what they truly mean. Our expectations, preconceptions, and own interpretation can be the source of misunderstanding and the source of most conflicts in relationships.

By being attentive and open to listen to ourselves, to others and our surroundings, we find a space of clarity, respect and understanding.

Sometimes people tell me, "You know what I mean." Actually, I don't know. I correct them and humbly admit that I don't know and would love to have more clarification about it.

It can be interesting to clarify with the other party what are their expectations. Clarify what they actually mean when they use the words 'prosperity', 'love', 'success', 'stress' and other words the meanings of which might be misconstrued. Be conscious of their interpretation and your own. Be in a clear state of mind.

On many occasions people have told me, "I didn't know you would think that way" or, "I didn't expect you to take what I said the way that you did." It has happened many times in my personal and professional experience that I have been very surprised to hear what the person truly thought and what their perception was about certain experiences. They have not always been able to clearly communicate what they meant and I have not always been listening carefully. Though when we choose to care, we give a space for mutual respect and clarification.

It is not only a language barrier. Rather, it is a different interpretation of the words. Our understanding or emotional connection or response to things that are said influence strongly our interpretation and understanding. Everyone hears things differently.

Some people begin to melt as soon as they hear the word 'love', while others receive a boost of confidence and feel stronger than ever. Many have different expectations in their relationships.

Can you accept the different perspectives and take them in consideration in your communication?

Acceptance doesn't mean that you give in and reverse your own opinion, rather that you respect everyone's opinions, needs and where they are on their own journey.

We are living in constant change and chaos. What was true yesterday may not be true today. By using the Elements in our communication, we lead the way towards truth, with clarity, compassion and direction.

Life can be perceived as a chaotic experience, with the movements, noises, environmental changes, as well as the changes in the community, the moods, the interests of the people who surround you. When we accept this sense of impermanence and listen attentively, we can direct our communication and attention in a way that will allow balance and integrity.

As I studied Handwriting Analysis, I discovered that there are clear psychological signs in the writers who are selective listeners. This can be a positive trait in some specific situations. However, it is a skill that has to be clearly managed in order to not fall into selective listening, an unconscious reflex triggered by leftover emotions or past traumas. You have to be attentive and develop the art of listening, in order to be clear in your communication.

Have you noticed that, on some occasions, there is a difference between what you actually hear, what you want to hear, and what the speaker really said?

In many situations we don't like what we hear and create our own interpretations in order to protect ourselves from a certain reality. We want to hear they aren't leaving us; they are just going out for a cup of coffee.

Our judgment can be hard and stressful on ourselves. In many circumstances, our own preconceptions can hurt us, even if the person speaking approaches us with a positive intention.

What do you say and what do you want to express? An angry father may say things to his child that he doesn't really mean. A stressed employee may speak to their boss in a way that is not appropriate. The emotional body influences our interpretations and communication. We will explore that aspect with more details in the Water Element, which deals with emotional intelligence.

We all create our own language and ways to express, to share, to ask questions. Many people say what they think the other person expects or wants them to say. Yet, in many circumstances, they try to fulfill non-existent expectations. *How do they know what the other person thinks and what the other person expects, when they have never clearly spoken about the subject together?*

Some people come for consultations and ask me what I think that the person they are upset about is thinking, as though I were a mind reader. How would I know if I have never met the other person? I explain that the best thing for them would be to sit together with the other person and clarify what they are thinking—without the need for guesswork or mind-reading. When we take the time to be attentive, to listen, we can notice that many times the person doesn't think or say what we thought they would.

What do you mean when you say, "I am frustrated at work"? Can you further develop that thought? *Is it a frustration because of the money or frustration because* of the inability to do what you like, or frustration for not being able to use your full potential, or is the communication with your colleagues not clear? Asking yourself questions until you have arrived at a clearer expression of your thinking can be a very helpful exercise. Putting some effort into the old adage, "Know Thyself" can be very rewarding.

When it comes to matters of the heart, can you clarify what your expectations are in a relationship?

What does love mean for you?

Where are you troubled? In which aspect of your life do you feel any stress? How does this stress manifest and how do you respond to it?

Do you equate how much money you make with success or do you have another perspective?

Taking some time to reflect on yourself can help you clarify your communication with others around you.

It happens on many occasions that we forget to clarify our understanding and communication. We build up preconceptions and judgments that are based on our own expectations, fears or attachments. So many times, we take conclusions based on a preconception without investigating deeper. There is no time or we are afraid to bother anyone or we are afraid of the reaction of the other person. Sometimes, there is a fear of conflict or even fear to get even more involved and therefore vulnerable and more exposed in our relationships.

It is always a relief when people "get you"—when they understand what you are saying and you needn't launch into a long explanation of everything you say in order to make yourself understood. To meet more of those types of like-minded people, you may first want to prioritize your own interests, using the Five Elements as a guide. The more you know about yourself, the more you can attract others who have similar interests or perspectives.

People have their mind set on different priorities and directions. Some are more interested in community and environment. Others focus their attentions and conversations towards their own family, status, goods, and benefits. Some people are more oriented towards the cultural aspects of life. Some are more interested in inner knowledge and the bigger spiritual questions, seeking for more reflection and understanding. Others are interested in adventure, always seeking new challenges and adopting hobbies, while others will be looking for quality time with friends and are most interested in nurturing emotional relationships. We can incorporate all these interests in our rich and full life.

How we use words to communicate about our lives is one important aspect of sharing ourselves with others. But our interpretation of any word comes from our education, experiences, memories and culture. We relate to a word and understand it through our emotional system.

Some people have discovered the word 'love' through experiences colored by kindness and joy. That will be the basis on which they understand the meaning of that word. Others will have had a different experience with that word and therefore a different interpretation. Yet we will be attracted towards relationships with people who perceive the word 'love' in ways that correspond to our own perception or in ways that complement it.

Other people have learned about 'love' filtered through aggression and stressful family situations. They will relate with that word from that level of comprehension and that will become their comfort zone. They will seek to be involved in that level of relationships.

This shows how our two nervous systems—our cerebral and enteric nervous systems—are connected. Our mind is intertwined with our emotional intelligence, which is why we experience gut feelings.

We want to respect everyone's interpretation and give him or her the opportunity to recognize his or her own perspective. This space of acceptance allows them to become aware of their attractions, expectations and choices. Acceptance and compassion supports the flow for evolution and opens the current for the changes to naturally occur. Resistance or denial inhibits the change and natural flow. Forcing change can cause another trauma and a sense of disconnection. Enabling a specific pattern or core belief can inhibit the process of evolution.

Everyone is right in his/her own way. We each can choose what is illusion and what is reality.

Reflection is an important tool to clarify where you are at this time of your life. Our perspective can be re-evaluated and reprogrammed through this holistic approach.

When you balance the Five Elements in your communication, you don't want to create any codependence with the people with whom you are conversing. You will allow space for independent thinking, for reflection and visualization. Everyone deserves respect and the freedom to think their way.

Whatever you choose to believe is and becomes your reality.

Juan was always responding from a place of stress, trying to be available for his clients and employees at any time. He trained them to expect his full attention for anything they may need or request. But he was beginning to be overwhelmed and couldn't be as available to answer all their questions immediately as he had been doing. His employees were neither taking responsibility nor doing their part in the process. He was not giving them space to clarify or allowing a pause that would give them a chance to reflect or to research a solution to their problems on their own before contacting him.

He learned that behavior from his past experiences, where he felt guilty for not having been available to some of his family members and friends in previous critical situations. Now, he was projecting that response mechanism on current communications and his relationships in general. As soon as Juan felt a slight twinge of guilt, he responded directly and immediately, going out of his way to do so. Though, when he became more mindful of this outdated belief, he began to create a distance between his emotions and actions and explored another perspective.

With time and experience in the following weeks, he noticed that he could be selective and clarify his communication. He noticed that some people began to respond surprisingly well to his new approach. It began to reflect his growing self-respect and his new respect for others.

 Expression and Leadership

In the Element of Fire, I take into consideration the ego and leadership necessary for conscious communication. It helps clarify our communication by bringing awareness of body language, expression and habits—both our own and others around us. We become more attentive to our feelings and the warmth and rhythm inherent in the interaction.

When we act from a space of confidence, clear in our expression, we allow a warm, uplifting interaction with others. Being centered and confident is contagious.

Do your actions reflect your words for a clear expression? How attentive are you to your feelings and those of others around you?

Our body language and expressions highly influence our communication. We can metaphorically burn ourselves or others, through our actions and the expression of our Fire Element. Some people may be very expressive, and extroverted, while others are more introverted. Both types of communicators deserve respect.

Being in tune with our feelings, and being sensitive to the feelings of others around us, is key for clear communication and to develop leadership skills.

A good leader considers the feelings and inspires people to develop their gifts and makes use of his or her own gifts in doing so.

When you communicate with someone, observe how he or she dresses, how he or she walks, sits and moves. The body language shows how he or she directs their actions, how conscious they are in their movement, expression, and interactions.

Through the expression and body language, you can learn a lot about a person. For more clarity, I organize fundamental aspects that are reflected in body language using the Five Elements.

The culture the person has grown up in or has lived with will show in their expression. It will be evident in the way they say "hello" and further revealed by the way they approach some subjects.

The intention of the person will be reflected in the way they act, move, dress and express themselves. It is an aspect that may take some time to explore and is not always immediately perceived. As you may know, sometimes appearances may lead to confusion.

Their main character traits will appear in the way they address others and in their actions. Their life's standards are something that can be discovered as you get to know the person better and get to know their habits.

You receive a sign in the first handshake. You can recognize what the person's main Element is at this time:

If the person you meet says "*hello*", with a light handshake and a distracted air (which may mean a flighty mind), they are in an airy mode. Your way to connect with them will be through clear expression, bringing their attention back to the topic, requiring them to be present and to keep their mind alert. Harness the power of the Element of Air.

When someone is proactive, dynamic and engaged in their way to say "hello", you may want to be attentive to the dynamic and clear expression, being attentive to the warmth and rhythm of the conversation. Fire is the Element in play.

Some people are very emotional and may even hug you on first meeting. Such an easy, smooth friendliness reflects certain sensitivity. Take into consideration that you are dealing with the Element of Water.

People who are firm, direct and assertive when they greet you are usually acting from a grounded space. They are inviting you to make commitment, are respectful of your time, space and boundaries, and pay strict attention to any status or hierarchy levels in play. With them you are dealing with the Element of Earth.

You can take these signs into consideration when communicating with a person. By paying attention to each person's significant character traits and their mood of the moment, you can better honor the Element at work.

Owning your role with clarity, intention, and determination yet being flexible while doing so, as opposed to appearing flighty, insecure or distant, will do much towards improving your communication.

Even in the way we walk, we can affect others around us and project a sense of strength, determination or weakness. It is no surprise that confident walkers rank near the bottom of potential crime victims.

Postural and gestural mirroring or mimicry is a sign of respect. It is always nice to see children's posture being so similar to their parents. The children learn from them and bond with them, gaining important lessons about respect. But you have to be careful not to copy someone exactly, which could be misinterpreted as mocking them. Take their posture into consideration, yet stay in a space of clarity and center.

Observe if the person is sitting straight. Do they have their arms and legs crossed or do they show an open expression?

Do they hold their hands on their hips, arms bent, showing confidence and assertiveness?

When you take in consideration the space and expression of everyone, you align your expression and create a healthy, respectful relationship. You will become more mindful of the rhythm in the communication, and understand your territorial nature, as well was the other person's. The personal space zone depends on the purpose and level of your relationship: 1½ feet for friendships (Water), 4-5 feet for professional or social encounters (Fire), 4-8 feet for cultural or consulting meetings (Air), less than 1 foot for intimate relationships (Earth).

If you notice that someone becomes too intrusive about your space and territory, you may want to find a way to respect healthy boundaries without appearing fearful or out of control. When you are mindful and clear in your communication, you will keep a healthy distance that is aligned with your intention. People will trust you when you are truly and genuinely in a posture of confidence, without trying to dominate or overwhelm the other party. This will reflect in the tone of your voice, in your expression and stature.

Relaxation is calmly powerful.

With time and experiences, we create a personality and an ego. We wear masks and identify with them. We fully believe in who we think we are. It requires attention, compassion and clarity to accept our beliefs and the role we have chosen to take into our lives. We choose our roles consciously or unconsciously.

Some people are extroverts and very expressive, relating easily with many people. Others are introverts, staying in their shell, keeping their feelings to themselves, sharing only with selective people at selective times.

When you relate with a person who is very expressive, strong in the Fire Element, you will be attentive in the way you direct your energy without burning out.

When you relate with a person who is introverted, your expression will have a different impact on their space and time. Your approach requires attention and consideration to stay pro-active, without being overly intrusive.

Also, you want to stay true to your own role and personality in your communication, expressing yourself with confidence.

Body language and expression are like a dance with the person with whom you are communicating.

Non-verbal communication occurs through gestures, such as a handshake, the way you hold your body, your sense of confidence. Being relaxed and alert is a position of power.

What do you choose to wear? The first impression counts. When you have a clear intention and you are attentive to your surroundings, you can dress in accordance. This will be an additional support to communicate clearly the message you want to share.

Steepling is a power gesture that reflects clarity and confidence. It is a position used by leaders in professional settings. In reflexology and mudras, this hand posture supports the balance between the right and the left-brain. It helps you to stay focused and centered.

Warmth and enthusiasm are skills that create warm (but not too hot) relationships. Enthusiasm and positive motivation are contagious.

When you create a clear decisive image asserting yourself with flexibility, it radiates competence.

If you try to dominate the situation, you may lose your leadership position and cause pressure in the communication. If you go into the other extreme, a lack of direction and leadership can cause doubts and a sense of abandonment.

We develop a healthy self-confidence when we develop a personality that is aligned with our vision, gifts and intention.

The motivation comes from our surroundings and environment, while the enthusiasm comes from our own inspiration, from within us. The motivation is more directed toward the goals and external directions. Enthusiasm should be directed towards the intention, reaching a state and space that is uplifting and shining from within.

The flame within us can shine with more radiance when there is uplifting and positive energy within and around us.

Our role and personality manifest in our form of expression. We can develop the skills to communicate and express clearly our will, vision, and mission. It takes determination and a sense of responsibility to train the muscles and lead our actions towards a clear direction.

It is almost like an acting class, where you learn to express yourself with integrity and purpose. There is a certain rhythm in the expression that brings warmth and motivation, as well as inspiration, to surround us.

"Creativity, based on freedom, and freedom based on responsibility, as in life, does not follow a rigid formula", wrote Uta Hagen in Respect for Acting.

We are the creators of our reality and it is our responsibility to nurture and encourage others to evolve and to shine as well.

Sometimes the excitement of the new can manifest like a spark, and shut down as fast as it lit up. A smooth fire can shine brighter and longer. Yet, the level and direction of the fire will respond to the intention and vision that require it to shine. The vision and direction of the mind is like the Air that gives the direction to the Fire. The sensibility is like the Water balancing its intensity. The discipline and support is represented by the Earth Element.

When you receive a gift nicely wrapped and accompanied by a big hug, you will appreciate it more than if the gift is left by the mailbox. The presentation and ways it is expressed add value to what you communicate.

Being a leader with a positive intention requires kindness, compassion, and well-meaning actions towards ourselves and our environment.

 Emotional Intelligence and Influence

The use of emotional intelligence is a skill that can be developed with time and dedication. For some people, it is a natural gift. Others may need more attention and focus to develop compassion, empathy, intuition and a clear sense of perception in their relationships.

There is a difference between emotions and feelings. I consider the emotions to be a part of the Water Element and feelings as part of the Fire Elements. Both are directly intertwined—so close, yet they are different.

Emotions flow by, while feelings begin to give direction, to spark an idea. It is when the emotions grow stronger that our feelings are touched. When we repress our emotions, we hold back our feelings. If we feel strongly for someone, we will open ourselves emotionally. Sometimes we begin by having a thought, an idea, and become so focused on it that it awakens feelings. These feelings will open the door to our emotional body, which can lead to a more emotional connection with the person or idea. All cycles of creation pass through emotions and are sparked by feelings.

Emotional intelligence takes into consideration our gut feeling. We do have a second brain in our gut, linked to the enteric nervous system. This is the one that responds to our intuition and sense of perception. Some people are more trained to use their psychological rational brain, while others are using more of the emotional intelligence. They both complement each other to support a balanced, mindful communication.

Before we can truly observe the emotional state of the others, we first have to be conscious of your own emotional state of being. Being aware of which emotion is triggered in a specific situation or through the tone of voice, expression and emotion or how someone important to us relates a story, will help us access our emotional body.

We attract, and are attracted by, some people and situations at specific times of our lives. There are no coincidences, rather causalities and synchronicities. Most of our attractions relate with some emotional sensations that we are familiar with, or that we seek consciously or unconsciously.

If you choose to communicate with mindfulness, honoring a positive intention, you will use emotional intelligence to support the well-being and evolution around you.

You want to master and channel your emotions with clarity and direction, to make sure that you won't become overly emotional through the process. But don't repress your emotions. They exist for a reason. Tune into your emotions and their expression. When you tune into your emotions, you are more empathic and can connect with others from the heart. Your intuition becomes stronger and you become more open to the other person's emotions.

You can use emotional states to facilitate creativity and problem solving. The emotions trigger the vital energy and bring more life and dynamism into your relationships.

You can learn to manage your emotions. Expressing emotional body language intelligently and strategically is the key. Yet, it happens often that we find ourselves overwhelmed by waves that we cannot always surf. We may crash a few times before we get to catch and to surf them with grace and intention. Never give up trying!

Most reactions—to fear, jealousy or anger—are dysfunctional. Those emotions are not negative, yet our own response and judgments about those emotions can transform them into a negative expression of feeling.

When we use our intuition, it is fundamental to use it wisely, as our intuition can be influenced by our emotional memories, preconceptions and subconscious expectations.

The other person will trust you if they notice that you are in tune with your emotions and if your expression is clear and sincere.

What is one of the main differences between emotions and feelings?

Emotions are like waves passing by, influenced by situations, people, and by our own thoughts. They respond to triggers that come from our environment or even from our own movements or state of mind. Feelings are more proactive, profoundly anchored and touch our heart. Emotions can develop into feelings when we begin to attach to them and express them outwardly.

When someone triggers emotions in you, generally you will begin to develop feelings for that person. If someone doesn't awaken any emotions, it will be difficult to have feelings.

Through life's experiences, we create and wear emotional masks. The repression of emotions and holding back what you really feel can bring misunderstanding. Each emotion has a unique expression, and when someone tries to mask them, we tend not to trust the person.

When we become more attentive to others around us, we can begin to recognize the expression of emotional states, such as nervousness, anger, numbness, hypersensitivity and happiness.

When we get closer to someone in our communication, we can recognize if there are acts of kindness or resistance that appear at specific times during the conversation. We can learn to take those aspects into consideration to improve communication. Also, it can be wise to resist categorizing people at a first meeting. When we allow a space for flexibility and we communicate from a space of clarity, free of expectations or judgment, we create space for growth and mutual respect.

When we are attentive to our emotional response, we notice how smells produce reactions. Many times they trigger memories related to that smell, taste, sight, sound, or touch. We have stored emotional memories that respond to external triggers. When we become more aware of our response mechanism, we can channel them with more awareness and intention.

Here are a few tips on how to develop emotional intelligence:

Understand the importance of emotional intelligence in all aspects of your life. You can journal daily to develop more self-awareness. Notice how you can improve self-management, directing your thoughts and channeling your emotions with clarity and intention.

Develop social awareness, observing your surroundings and being conscious of your social environment. Develop communication skills to manage and nurture healthy relationships.

With dedication, you will get stronger and face situations of conflict or confrontation with compassion and confidence. Remember that everyone has a different perspective and comes from different life experiences. Through life experiences only, we can learn to recognize stress triggers and how to deal with stress. It is not just a theory. Sometimes we can understand it clearly with our mind, or so it appears. Yet, it is not until we fully face life's experiences, that we can develop the emotional intelligence necessary to truly understand. Developing an open mind, being curious, agreeable and empathetic is key.

It is as when you learn to surf the waves of emotions and life. You can learn to read the waves and catch the waves only with direct experience. You may crash a few times before you can manage. It is not by running away that you will learn. Be aware that you don't have to continuously crash in the same way, over and over again. This can become a comfort zone and not give you a chance to develop your potential. You may have to be selective and focus on one lesson at a time, rather than taking too much in, which won't give the opportunity to grow stronger step-by-step.

You have to turn and flow just before the peak of a wave to develop more strength and clarity, step-by-step, until later, when your confidence grows and you can access a higher level, channeling the power of the emotion with clarity and bliss.

Instead of running away from situations of conflict or stressful circumstances, we can face those with mindfulness, being prepared to deliberate. If we constantly run away from stressful situations, we don't really run away from the situations or people seemingly causing us trouble. We run away from our own emotions, our own expression and the possibility to develop our emotional potential.

Sharing quality time is key to bonding and growing a relationship. The emotional support is key for evolution in our relationships. Most people's education has been nurtured by negative attention. We usually give attention towards people who have problems, who have difficulty, who need support. We haven't learned to give attention to people who are doing well or to those who are creative and inspired.

I was working with a woman who had difficulty with her family and in her relationship with her husband. She was thinking that it was maybe the time to divorce or at least to separate. Yet, what she discovered was that she had to divorce and detach from her commitment to her ego, core beliefs and emotional attachments and expectations. When she began to let go of that strong fear and attachment, and focused on healthy values and positive intention, she noticed that her relationship with her husband and family became more harmonious and pleasant. She began to nurture the positive aspects in her relationship. The more she focused her attention towards those positive signs, the more they expanded and grew. The previous problems grew small in comparison to all the other aspects she began to let grow into a harmonious, inspiring relationship.

We do have emotional boundaries and begin to recognize those as we develop more sensitivity towards ourselves and our surroundings.

Welcome your emotions. They lead you to access the source of your creative expression.

Daniel told me one day that he didn't know much how to speak and what to speak about with his sister anymore. They spoke often when both were passing through difficult times and had problems in their lives they could share. But, once things improved, they didn't seem to know what to talk about anymore. They had to learn a new language and create a different level in their interaction. They did and began to share creative expression.

When we change our point of reference and perspective we are learning a new language, a new way to relate with ourselves and with others. It requires creativity and dedication to develop this new way to share and communicate. In order to access this creative energy, we have to open to the flow of emotion. It is like a valve of water that you can open to allow the circulation of the creative expression.

We may have learned that if we are doing well and feeling balanced, we will then be alone or dismissed. When someone is doing well and doesn't receive the same level of attention they did when they were beset by problems, they may subconsciously feel punished for doing well. *Why is the other person, who doesn't pay their bill and declares bankruptcy, not always called to task?* It seems they get more support an attention than the other people who work very hard, pay their bills and fully respond to their responsibilities.

Why do the people who care a lot about their health not receive a lower rate for their health insurance that those who don't care about their diet, lifestyle, and wellbeing? Why aren't we supporting the healthy people in their quest to stay healthy?

Everyone deserves attention and respect. It is a natural reaction to feel punished if we don't receive any appreciation for doing something good. As human beings, we all need a minimum level of emotional support, whether we feel good or bad.

We can support and give attention to people around us, as well as ask attention even when all is good. That way we can inspire each other to be even better.

To use emotional intelligence wisely is to not use stress, fear or intrusion to influence the people around us. Rather we prefer to inspire and motivate them to grow and relate from a healthy, nurturing place. Some people use pressure and threats to try to make a person move or change. *Is that really necessary or can we find a more compassionate way to inspire growth and development?*

What brings you happiness? Is the need for instant gratifications nurturing your happiness? Sometimes it does, yet most of the times it doesn't.

Honoring healthy values in the development of a vision and clear relationships is key for a balanced lifestyle. When we notice that the water becomes choppy or dirty, it means that it is time to bring more calm and clear it. It is the same in relationships. When we notice that some emotions becomes unpleasant and that we become more moody, it means that it is time to clarify our communication. We may have to consider which emotions are being triggered, what is the trigger, and how to restore balance before it becomes too intense or overwhelming to be managed.

In my own experience, I noticed that nurturing healthy relationships, whether that is with my family, clients, community, environment and my own thoughts is the main key for happiness. When I resist or fight an emotion, it creates an inner conflict and pulls me away from my intended focus. Even if the emotion is anger or frustration, learning to relate to these emotions and channeling them with intention can nurture happiness.

When we have deep emotions coming up, it usually speeds up our heart rate. When I was immersed with shamans in South America, we used the drums to reflect heartbeats, and the symbol of the horse walking or galloping. Tuning into those drum rhythms brought me into profound connection with my heart center.

When I guided Jasmine through the DHARMI Map, she described how lost she felt at a time of her life where she experienced a profound loss in her family. She shared that her heart was beating very fast when she opened the expression of her sadness and emotions. She said she was afraid to lose herself and was trying to resist those deep emotions. Through a guided meditation, I suggested she connect with the fast-paced heartbeats and breathe deeply. I encouraged her to focus her mind as if she was horseback riding, and her horse (heart) was galloping fast. She was staying on the horse, breathing, learning to hold on to a profound connection with her heart. After a few breaths, and with clear focus, she felt a deep relief through her whole being. She said, "*I feel safe and at home*".

As a child, I lived in the countryside and sometimes had the chance to be on a horse. A lesson I learned was that if I was thinking I was lost, or the horse was beginning to be out of my control, I had to hold on. The horse would always bring me home if I just held onto it. Later on, through the shamanic experiences, playing the drum with the symbol of the horse, it reminded me of that time. The drum, the heartbeats, the horse, will still always bring me home.

Manifestation, Sense of Space and Ownership (Earth)

In the Earth Element, we respect the space and time of each party. We consider the foundation, the common ground that we can create for a clear communication.

That base is like the container that will support and allow the expression, growth and development of your relationship. In order to support others, you need to have a good discipline and healthy lifestyle yourself. Your own well-being and balance will show that you care.

The foundation and structure are important. They allow you to respect the resources, to value the capital of vital energy of the person with whom you can relate. Remember to value your time and the time of others. Provide space, structure and a clear frame and methodology. Have a clear discipline and ethics, and share them with the other person involved in the relationship.

Prosperity doesn't only mean having money. It means having resources of time, space, economy, experience, and relationships. In some situations, the emotional capital is as important and can be even more important, than the financial capital.

In the Earth Element, we build a capital of resources, of experience, of relationships and of confidence that will support well-being and evolution. You will consider the foundation of the person you relate with, the culture they live in, the education they have received and the land and family from which they come.

I had the chance to travel through five continents and work with people, leading them through the Map. In order to share with people from different cultures, different perspectives, and different traditions, I had to establish a certain connection and foundation with their reality. By having a good foundation and following a clear discipline myself in all those different forms and realities, allowed me to support them with clarity and objectivity. I learned to be a survivor, to find resources and solutions in many critical situations myself. The fact that I had to deal with surviving and harnessing energy gave me the strength to support them to access their own base.

The energy of the Earth asks us to go deep in the roots of our being and bring flexibility, together with strength, in our discipline, organization and management.

People coming from Europe will have a different way to relate than people from the United States or Asia. Our traditions, education and the environment we are coming from affect us in our values, ethics, and priorities.

In Switzerland, if we have an appointment at 2 pm, we arrive at 1:55 pm. In Argentina, I was invited for tea at 5 pm. I arrived at 5 pm and it was considered impolite. I had to arrive 30 minutes after an appointment to be on time.

Time and space management have to be adapted to the culture and circumstances, as I discussed previously. Yet, honoring your own way, your own truth, time and space is a key aspect that can provide credibility. A clear communication gives the possibility to find a common ground where the parties involved can relate with harmony and respect.

During the time I lived in South America, I offered my services in a holistic center in Santiago de Chile for a year. The people at the center asked me how I was arranging it that my clients came on time for their appointments. The other professionals who worked at that place didn't have their clients arrive on time. I reminded them that I am Swiss, not only in my nationality, but in my expression and in my foundation. People feel and see it in my posture, in my voice and communication that I appreciate punctuality. My clients and I organized the schedule and found common ground with mutual respect. I kept my commitment to them and, by and large, they kept theirs to me.

It is only once we clearly determine the value of our time and clarify our boundaries and path that we can be assertive, respect it and have it respected. Giving it space for flexibility is helping in your communication and negotiation with others. Yet, being too flexible can make you lose your ground and lose the deal.

Inspiration-Liberation

In this step, I consider the synchronicities and the leaps of faith. We do have to surrender to be and surrender to what is.

When we accept that life is a constant evolution, we surrender to the moments and experiences without attachments or unexpressed expectations. We become more attentive to the synchronicities and opportunities that appear on our day-to-day life.

As much as we like to be in control, mindful and masters of our life, there is still a mystery, a higher plan that we don't always see. Allowing a space for life's wonders to unveil themselves and accepting that things occur for us to learn lets the surprising plan manifest before our eyes.

We learn to navigate those changes with as much compassion, acceptance and bliss as we can.

Many times, there are things in life we don't understand.

Why a young woman who doesn't want a child just yet finds herself pregnant from an abusive relationship, while another woman who is in a loving relationship have been trying to be pregnant for four years, and yet nothing has happened.

Why someone who has a beautiful vision for the community doesn't have the resources to make it manifest, while another person, with destructive behaviors, has access to unlimited resources.

Sometimes we may feel guilty for having such a beautiful life, full of possibilities, while others are much less fortunate.

We learn that we cannot compare, we can just live the best we can, honoring our truth and responding to our own destiny with positive intention.

In our communication it is the moment of 'pause', that which gives us space. It opens possibilities and allows us to meet and face some new situations and people with equanimity.

There is something that is there, beyond our control and above our understanding. That spiritual space deserves to be honored. The synchronicities and signs on our journey are there to guide our steps. It is very humbling to listen to that Higher Purpose, to that truth that is out of our hands, yet fully in our own hands. It is our responsibility to fulfill this destiny. No one else can do it for us. It is not better, neither less than anyone else's. It just is what is.

When we have a dream or inspiration, we can keep it as a dream, holding on to it. This won't allow us to explore further than it. When we follow and manifest a dream, we open the door to another dream. It allows us to unveil life's wonders, opening the portals in the labyrinth.

Practice detachment for a clear connection in your communication. Create a space to release expectation and to honor what is.

Below, I share with you some examples on how to apply a full cycle through the Elements in communication.

Here is a report that I received from a person, who was learning to apply conscious communication into her life:

When Julie joined a yoga class, she met a new participant, who spontaneously set up her mat close to Julie's. She was so close that it was agitating Julie. In fact, the woman seemed unpleasant, not even saying hello and showing no interest in her environment. She didn't even smile. Her face and body looked very tight.

But Julie began a plan of conscious communication between herself and the woman, using these touchstones:

Approach

At the end of the class, as they were clearing up the space, the teacher directed Julie towards the new student, saying she, like Julie, was also French. Julie felt obligated to engage a conversation with her. And at that exact moment, as she was saying the first word to this stranger, Julie thought that it would be a very good opportunity to apply the tools that she had learned through a seminar on how to integrate the Elements in Communication.

Presence

Immediately she brought awareness in her own presence. She took a deep breath and linked to a centering space. As Julie opened her mind, the first impressions and apprehensions that she had disappeared completely. It gave her the opportunity to initiate the relationship again. This time Julie did it without any preconception.

She clarified her intention to 'be mindful' and share a short conversation without expectations.

Listening with Understanding and Comprehension

During the conversation, Julie was very attentive to what was being said. The two women spoke on basic subjects. As it was their first encounter, Julie chose to not go too deep in the process of discovering facts about the woman. She didn't want to be intrusive or inquisitive. She learned that the woman's name was Patricia. She learned that she had moved to United States a few months ago with her family and other main aspects in a first conversation.

Body Language

During the conversation, Julie noticed that Patricia was beginning to calm down. Her body appeared less tight and she seemed more relaxed, finally sitting down. Julie chose to sit down as well. It didn't feel comfortable to stay upright, so she mirrored her body posture to a point that would allow more ease and flow in her communication. The newcomer's face began to soften and she began to open up. She appeared younger and began to smile. As both women stood up to leave the room, it appeared to Julie that Patricia was standing taller.

Sharing, Intuition, Emotional Intelligence

Both women felt comfortable, at ease with each other. Julie was very impressed that she could change the first impression she had gotten of the new student.

This change of perception came by Julie's willingness to enter in a relationship with 'mindfulness'.

Julie had utilized a mutual respect of both women's space and time. They exchanged numbers after noticing that they both had similar points of reference on some basic things like family, children, and the problems presented by transitioning into a new country.

Emotional Support, Positive Attention

Julie felt that her new friend was very concerned about the education of her children and about the cultural differences that she was facing since she had arrived in United States. Julie could relate to her and shared her vision about it, as she was also concerned about similar subjects concerning her children and family. Their values were aligned in many aspects.

Motivation, Leadership As Julie shared her own vision and gave Patricia some attention, she felt that, "I brought some inspiration into her day".

Clarity, Liberation

Julie hopes they may meet again soon and is leaving herself open to possibilities.

Below is the example of the application of the Five Elements in communication in a business relationship.

Robert was meeting a new potential client. He had a clear intention and was open to this opportunity. He noticed that he already had many expectations, being eager to complete a sale and sign a valuable contract.

Yet, he chose to honor his values and to be clear in his communication.

As Kathy (the potential client) was in town only for a few days, her assistant organized a meeting at Robert's showroom at a specific time.

When Kathy arrived, she and Robert introduced themselves. He was attentive to her expression. In his first observation, he noticed strong characteristics of the Earth and Fire Elements. She reflected confidence and it looked like she was standing strong on her ground. He took this aspect into consideration and chose to lead the conversation to the main reason of her visit. Robert asked her how he could help her, to clarify what she was looking for and for what purpose.

Kathy was looking for furniture to decorate the new home of one of her clients, who had bought a property in the city.

Robert asked her if there is any specific style her client was looking for.

She answered that what he had in his showroom was very much aligned with what her client was looking for to furnish her new home. Kathy came personally to make sure that the quality of Robert's wares was going to correspond to her client's needs. Yet, despite liking the style, she was a little concerned with what she was seeing and the quality of the goods.

Robert had different styles of furniture. However, he focused more on accessible pieces, rather than high-end products. He chose to honor his values. He told her he could provide her with similar styles in a better quality and with a higher-end presentation. But he related that it might take a few more weeks to have them available. He asked her, by when do they need the furniture?

Kathy told him that they are doing construction at her client's new home and she would need the furniture in four-to-six weeks.

Robert noticed by her expression she was keeping some distance. So he engaged more by telling her about some of the furniture he has sold six months ago to a high-end client. He shared how the process went well and even had pictures to show to her in his portfolio of how the final presentation looked in their home. He engaged some more Fire and injected warmth in the interaction. As the home looked really beautiful, clear and very well-presented, a spark of motivation appeared in Julie again.

Their conversation began to enter in a space of creativity, where they shared ideas and possibilities. This sharing time opened the flow in their relationship and allowed a space of connection and bonding. As both were inspired to work together on that project, Robert suggested her to clarify the conditions on how they will work together. She made a suggestion and they both had to find a common ground before going any step further.

It was only after that base and structure was strong, that they could begin to move on with the project.

They have passed through a first cycle through the Five Elements in their communication. He was glad that they could already go so far.

By being attentive to her body language, Robert inspired Kathy to continue the meeting.

He integrated the Elements, taking time to clarify precisely what were her expectations (Air). He found a way to inspire her and act in a direction that motivated her to work together with him (Fire). He considered her sensitivity and also his own, honoring healthy values and being honest in offering her only those furnishing he could procure (Water). In the Earth Element, he set a clear condition to look for a common ground in their timing to manifest this project together (Earth).

We always consider all the Elements, yet we may focus more attention and time on the ones that are the most relevant at the time.

At the completion of those first steps, Robert suggested she clarify how many items and of which style would best suit her clients' taste and their budget. That way he could do some research and they agreed to meet the next day at a specific time to review his suggestions, before he prepared a proposal for her. In this way, they both had space and time to reflect.

He did some research and they had another meeting the next day, where she chose specific items and clarified her request. Robert took into consideration the Elements in their communication again during that meeting, so he could prepare a clear proposal for her.

The following steps were in between Earth and Water. They had taken the steps engaging Earth and Water, allowing a time to prepare the base, negotiate, and clarify conditions, timings and values.

The next steps began after their full agreement of the project and proposal.

When the base was clear, they needed a close relationship to update each other on the development of the project and its timing, to make sure that the construction and delivery schedule of the furnishings jibed.

In the Fire Element, this was the moment of action, which required coordination and a clear direction.

In the Air Element, it was the moment of final delivery, the completion of the service that was agreed. They made sure that all aspects have been completed, that the quality of the products responded to what was planned, before letting go (in the Ether).

Robert and Kathy followed these steps with clarity and integrity in the manifestation of their visions.

The tools that Robert has used in his communication supported him to lead the project and business relationship with mindfulness. He was aware of the needs of his client. Robert set up clear conditions and timings (*Earth*) that were aligned with his values (*Water*) and Kathy's and her client's desires (*Fire*). That way, the delivery (*Air*) could happen with clarity.

As all the elements were aligned some synchronicities appeared through the project. Such as:

The constructions took one more week than planned, which was the exact extra time that Robert needed for their order to be well completed and shipped to the client.

Robert had some bills due that were difficult for him to cover, in order to keep his showroom open. This job brought him the money he needed, and the confidence to pursue his vision, while he was honoring his values.

We recognize clearly synchronicities when we are conscious and alert.

To learn more about how to utilize these steps, support the process, facilitate the manifestation of your project or to clarify your communication in any specific relationship, please feel free to contact one of our licensed consultants. Reach us at info@dharmi.com.

- DHARMI MAP -

CHAPTER SIX
The Elements for Balance and Healing

Integrating the Elements for Balance & Healing

There are different layers that intertwine. Often, when there is difficulty in communication, relationships, self or business development, it can be in direct connection to more profound aspects in our own well-being and inner space.

Often, when there is an imbalance in one aspect, it may reflect in many other aspects of your life while being a reflection or response from one specific Element.

Here is an example from a client of mine I will call John.

John was possessed of great creativity, particularly in his social skills and the way he communicated with others. But he found it difficult to order his thoughts and express them clearly, which prevented him from expressing himself fully and meeting like-minded people with whom he shared much in common. He began to integrate mindfulness in his communication and set more clear direction and began concentrating in his thought process.

Such disorganization in his thinking led him to have difficulty with his finances, particularly in the area of paying his bills on time. This affected his credit and credibility, negatively affecting his business relationships. When he began to integrate the Elements in his business, he noticed that very little of his attention was dedicated to the foundation, organization and framework of his team and business. He contacted the right person to support him in the organization of the foundation, time and resources with clarity.

In John's emotional relationships, he felt somewhat oppressed, as though his space were being invaded. This made for a certain distance between him and his partners, leading to sexual difficulty for him and an inability to satisfy his partner and his own needs and desires. When he began to approach his relationship and emotional aspect with a holistic perspective, he could integrate more of a common ground and pass through emotional boundaries that were holding him back. He noticed the taboo that had been built around pleasures, basic human needs and intimacy.

This imbalance manifested itself physically as well. A visit to a medical practitioners revealed John's hips were misaligned. His worries lead to trouble sleeping which was exacerbated by his feeling of being cramped. Neither was the situation helped by his being inability to stick to a regular bedtime schedule due to his lack of discipline. When we observed his foundation, lifestyle and well-being, he noticed that he could bring more attention to a healthy discipline, bringing more nurturing in his lifestyle, respecting his time, body and space. This required focus and perseverance.

All of John's troubles directly related to the Element of Earth. He needed grounding, centering and healing. His life was off-balance as was reflected in his body. John needed to be made aware that the conflicts and imbalances from which he suffered were not isolated experiences. They were all connected to a mental, physical and emotional misalignment and all could be corrected by addressing the source via healing, nurturing and balancing Earth Element.

I supported him to be mindful in integrating the Earth Element in all aspects of his life. This supported an integrative process of development. When he began to align this Element in his lifestyle, business, and emotional relationships, his own health began to improve. His hips were more aligned, as he was becoming more grounded, aligned and true to his path and his needs through the day.

Here is another example where you will notice the interconnectedness and reflection of a specific imbalance in different aspect of somebody's life:

Cary was a young woman who appeared to have it all together. She had a good job, a busy social life with plenty of friends, enough money to dress well, dine out and take vacations. But she felt lethargic, bored and often tired. She felt no spark within, and therein lay the clue to her malaise. Cary didn't finish what she started. Her interest waned after a few months. Cary thought she would like a different job, but couldn't drum up the commitment to search for a new position. Neither did she know where to direct her attention. She didn't pursue a fulfilling romantic relationship, covering over her own desires and feelings so well she was barely aware of having them anymore. She smoked and quit several times, only to abandon the resolution when she began to feel better. She knew she was harming her health and well-being, yet she couldn't summon the fortitude to quit permanently.

In all ways, Cary was smothering her own fire. Her feelings had been hurt and her self-confidence damaged by incidences earlier in her life. She repressed her Fire Element in an attempt to tamp down the feelings aroused by those past hurts. She was literally kicking dirt onto her bonfire. What Cary didn't know, until we began our work together with the DHARMI Map, is that a true Fire doesn't go completely out for a good long while after it looks as though it has. There are embers underneath, waiting to roar back to life with just a little fuel. Cary needed her embers stirred as they were waiting to uplift her spirit again.

Lately, her focus has been in nurturing her Earth and Air, using her rational mind to collect more material wealth and security. She didn't have much space or time to clarify her desires (Fire) and to nurture her relationships (Water).

During certain rituals during my time with the shamans of Central and South America, some of us in attendance were charged with keeping the fire burning during many days of ceremony. We organized a circle of firekeepers. If one of us was falling asleep during his or her watch, imperiling the fire and causing it to almost die down, we had to find a way to light it up again from the embers still alive underneath the ashes.

In our lives, we can forget to nurture our own fires, distracted by our lives and problems. We risk having our fires die down and even die out. Noticing the fire has gone after the last ember has flickered out is too late. We must search for that spark while it remains and, by our efforts, fan its small light into a warming beacon of hope. Such work will take time, but if we apply ourselves, we, like the fire, will grow strong and shine brightly again.

I began my career in holistic healing and therapies in 1990 in Switzerland. My work in consulting and mentoring came along later, after years of working with many people and studies and research in different cultures. I became ever more aware of the interconnectedness between the Elements in all aspects of our lives.

For an integrative process of development, it is fundamental to take into consideration both aspects of the alignment—those within and around us.

If we try to change our work and our relationships without considering our inner journey, the task is futile. We will continue to be attracted to and attract similar situations. We will find we don't have the tools to deal with a new form of business or different way of nurturing our relationships.

If we try to change ourselves from within, we will be able to heal traumas and release attachments. Without such organization of the reality around us, we will find we are adrift, unable to steer our choices, whether those are in our professional direction or relationships. We will create a gap that can grow bigger with time, exasperating our sense of disconnectedness and causing frustration, as the same problems need to be faced again and again. Scabs are torn off old wounds only to grow again and be again torn off in a painful cycle without end.

Yet, the day you clarify your intention, values and gifts, you will nurture them and empower them in all Five Elements. A natural selection and shift will happen around you and your daily life will reflect that change. From that healthy nurtured form of expression, the scab falls off naturally, whenever the wound is healed enough. It may remain a scar as a reminder and mark of wisdom. However, the healing can happen while strengthening the immune system, building a new skin, a new potential and a new perspective.

I present different ways to heal and balance the Elements, such as holistic foot analysis, dance therapy, mandala creation, healing/touch, meditation, journaling and yoga. Another book will be specifically dedicated to DHARMI-YOGA with the integration of the Elements in the practice and philosophy for holistic development. These serve only an introduction to the various modalities that can be integrated into your life to support your holistic development. This information and these practices are not intended as vehicles for self-healing. I highly recommend you to contact a professional if you like to experience any of them in a clear and effective way.

Being fearful of decision-making or inability to focus your attention on a task can be left over from a trauma we suffered in our childhood. Or they may stem from a learning experience, whether physical or emotional, firmly rooted in our body, memory and heart that deeply hurt us. From such experiences we draw conclusions, building up core beliefs in our subconscious mind. But we can also choose to heal those wounds, search for a space of balance, learn from a space of wisdom and treat ourselves with compassion and clarity.

Returning to Cary's experience, she discovered after a few consultations, that she was attached to patterns of behavior that were causing her harm. She was focusing strongly on a linear way of thinking, looking for happiness in material achievements and successes. It was giving her more stability and security, yet she was distracted from her intention, values and profound inspirations. This behavior, so long ingrained, favored her sense of control. After she became more mindful of the behavior, she found she could detach from it and see that it was not allowing her own self-expression. The control she was attached to was holding her back from any new possibilities or development. In the next few weeks she still held on that control, yet was doing it with more space and flexibility. This kept her in a safe place, while opening new doors with care and clarity. She became aware that the part of her that took initiative and action has been weakened over time, as the sense of control holding her back was getting stronger. As she was more mindful, she began to pay more attention to her ability to initiate action towards interests and hobbies she had procrastinated for a long time and found gratification in doing so.

She began to be more attentive to her desires, opening her mind to dream, to think further and look deeper. What was at first an effort, soon became more natural in the following weeks.

It takes attention, mindfulness and a certain level of commitment to nurture an intention, reflect on it, and then manifest it with harmony and integrity. At the beginning, it is like a new muscle we try to use, stiff and unfamiliar at first, but growing ever stronger through use. Practice does make perfect and practicing using such intention in your mind, your everyday actions, the way you channel your emotions and your sense of direction helps that intention to manifest. Trying something new, with a new approach that is in tune with a positive intention, is leading you the right way.

In some places, when a baby elephant was trained, they attached a rope around his foot. As soon as he tried to pull away, the rope tightened, and an electric shock was administered. The shock immediately stopped him in his tracks and soon no electricity was needed at all. The presence of the rope alone and the slight pressure exerted when he pulled away was enough to have him stop and return to the desired position. He had learned obedience through muscle and pain memory.

We humans learn the same way, starting in early childhood, or some say even since the time of our conception. We develop fears and pain-body responses. We may be fully grown, mature adults and yet, a picture, a piece of music or a random thought can reduce us to tears or resurrect old fears in an instant and make them feel as fresh as if the wound had just happened.

Another person I have guided through the Map, Terri, was a healthy intelligent and wealthy woman. She had lived a life filled with travels, rich in experiences and encounters in social, cultural, and educational aspects. She had been married for 30 years. Yet, because of a trigger from her past, where a loved one left, Terri thought her life was the worst in the world. She felt as though she was barely surviving, her condition critical. When this emotion took her over completely, she forgot about all other beautiful aspects of her life and could see and feel only the pain. It took some time of reflection, meditation and re-evaluation for her to complete the cycle and for her to reach a space of clarity. Once done, she found again her inner strength and balance.

The core belief, "I have no reason to live" and hurtful question, "What am I doing here?" had been screaming so loudly that her self-esteem was smashed. Her feelings were constantly hurt by the wailings of her loud ego, which acted as a protective mechanism when she felt a loss in her life. As Terri accessed a space of strength and confidence within herself, she could recognize when that hurtful ego was coming up. She found a new strength that was located in the area of her thymus and throat. From that point of reference and with the intention of strength, she began to find the energy to stay in her heart while facing difficult situations. That voice still arose sometimes, but its intensity was diminished and no longer interfered with her daily obligations and priorities.

Step-by-step, strengthened by her new perspective, Terri began to build up a life that was more aligned with her tastes, interests and values. She began to feel worthy to shine and to listen to her own feelings. She allowed some space for her own needs and desires to be fulfilled while still honoring healthy values and caring for others around her.

Phases in Self-Development

First we are unconscious and therefore incompetent. At that time, we are not aware of certain patterns, core beliefs or our response mechanisms. We may choose to deny or distance ourselves from any situations or people that may hurt our ego. It feels comfortable to us to run from the pain. We may not notice that we are incompetent in some areas, as those aren't presently bothering us, so we haven't even taken them into consideration.

We may receive new opportunities or challenges that show us that we are actually incompetent in some areas. We can choose to become conscious of such failings and grow from them or we can choose to procrastinate, about learning the lessons or even deny there are any lessons necessary for us to learn.

We can choose to enter into denial about any uncomfortable or unknown situation or face that aspect, being willing to develop that potential. In this step, we explore which potential, which aspect in our being, is calling for attention and development. We choose to learn from life's lessons and continue a process of self-development, or hold back and choose to stay in our comfort zone.

We can develop skills, step-by-step, on our journey. It is in our nature to change, to evolve, to awaken new possibilities, perspectives and approaches in our lives. Who we think we are may be who we learned we were. Yet, we are constantly learning and evolving. Our life is filled with wonders that we can explore and potential we can awaken.

This is usually when we look for a neutral external support, which provides tools to lead us towards the next step. Or we look for a company or person who has the expertise in the field or aspects that we are seeking to understand. We are aware that something is not working or that it could be improved. We are willing to act upon it and take responsibility to explore that other dimension.

After evaluation, consideration and reflection, we begin to develop competency and to unveil new perspectives. We can consciously become competent. This means that we have to be attentive and focus our attention. We must incorporate a new attitude and take action for our potential to be developed. It takes an effort to stay in that new perspective and act from that positive intention with integrity. Synchronicities begin to appear on our path when this happens, giving us the opportunity to channel our attention and energy wisely.

We enter into being competent unconsciously. It is when such competence becomes second nature that it becomes more familiar and comfortable to act and relate from this new point of reference. This is when we feel like we are living in the right place and time.

For example, if a woman had never heard of yoga and breathing techniques, she wouldn't be aware of what skills and abilities could develop by adopting the practice. She wouldn't know of the benefits such a yoga practice could bring to her life, nor does she any lack without it. She is not aware that she could feel any better than the way she feels now.

One day she came across a video online of pranayama (yoga breathing technique). It was five minutes of basic exercise. This first experience brought her energy right away and a profound relief of her stress. She noticed in the next few days that the meditation and mindful breathing practice could support her to feel better, though, she went back into her stressful approach to her everyday life shortly thereafter. She explored no new possibilities.

That is the point of decision, the key Element in all process of development. Are you going to step back into your comfort zone, or are you willing to pursue a new outcome? Our newcomer could decide to attend more classes, ask for help from the teacher and practice regularly. With such focus, conscious determination and attention, she could develop new potential.

Later on, certain Elements of compassion and focus, as well as some asanas (yoga postures) will become like second nature to her.

How can you explore the Five Elements more profoundly on your inner journey in a way that may affect all other aspects that surround you? By examining your core beliefs, observing your forms of expression, being sensitive to your emotions, attentive to your needs and aligned with a clear intention is how.

Clearing the energy within us will give us more clarity, strength, and compassion to deal with our environment, our loved ones, inspirations and community.

When we face a big wall, concerning our life's situations or relationships, it is an invitation to look inside, to access our values and to test our new potentials. It is the chance to clarify our position and role, as well as our priorities and perspectives.

In response to any given situation, each person will react differently based on the beliefs he or she has created and projected. The person's perspective, projection and reflection influence themselves and their environment.

Each reaction will be manifested by the following aspects:

> A belief (*Air Element*)
>
> An active expression and feeling (*Fire Element*)
>
> An emotional response (*Water Element*)
>
> A physical sensation (*Earth Element*)
>
> An intention (*Ether Element*)

The terms "*intelligence memory*" and "*DNA programming*" refer to the way that our cells reflect our personal history. To be more specific, our intelligence memory retains the reactions and conclusions we take from our experiences. Scientific research has produced proof that our emotional memories are reflected in our physical cells. There is an emotional coding to the way our autonomic patterns are elaborated. Many aspects that are imbalanced can be approached, and the weak area can be strengthened, through the three pathways in the DHARMI Map.

In the different DHARMI pathways, we always consider a holistic approach based on the Five Elements and Seven Tonalities or in voices of the mind, of the heart, of the emotions, of the physical body, the DNA/lineage, the spiritual and the connective energy. For the process to be fully holistic and integrated, we cannot consider only one of the pathways, The Elements. We also consider the Cycles of Evolution and the Resonance.

Main Stages in Life

The stages in life are from Conception to Birth and from Birth to Evolution.

In reference to holistic foot reflexology, the moment of conception is reflected in the area of the jaw, the big toe and the occipital area of our cranium.

When we work with craniosacral therapy, we balance the nervous system and fascia tissue, healing traumas that were received from conception to birth, as well as those gained through life's evolution.

The base of the cranium, where a specific nerve flow may be affected, is located in the area where a foot would reveal the moment of conception and is the time period to be examined. The sacrum (the other area referenced during craniosacral therapy) is where we observe the moment of birth. The process from conception (crania) to birth (sacrum) is where are held the most fundamental memories—the ones that will influence the rest of our lives.

Running down along the inner edge of the foot, we follow the different stages through the time of gestation.

The birth, the completion of the cycle of gestation, is in the area of the sacrum reflected in the heel of the foot.

We see the father figure and his influence reflected in the right foot. This side represents the social and rational aspects of our life, the ones that causes us to be proactive and take charge, moving confidently into the future.

The mother side appears on our left foot. This represents our intuitive and emotional side, that which affects our relationships—intimate and otherwise.

After our birth, we advance through the process of growth and evolution, passing through the Elements:

Baby to child (*Birth to 4 years*): Here we encounter our survival instinct and form our foundation. This is the Earth Element.

Child (*From 4 years to 12 years*): This time is dominated by the development of our emotional intelligence, finding emotional detachment and independence while learning to deal with emotions. This is the Water Element.

Teenager (*12 to 20 years old*): We are developing our personality and forming the foundation of our identity. This is the development of the willpower and self-confidence in the Fire Element.

Adulthood (*from 20-26 years*): Here we choose our focus and what will absorb our attention. We develop our psychological potential and become independent thinker. This is the Air Element.

After the age of 26, many people continue to repeat cycles, and apply what they learned in those first years.

By using this timeline, we can recognize if there have been specific traumas or choices we have made along the way, which continues to influence us in our daily life, whether we are conscious or unconscious of that influence. The more aware we become, the better we can direct our attention, heal our wounds, and take responsibility for our actions and decisions.

Yet, you can choose to complete cycles instead of repeating cycles – avoid just turning in circles. You can learn to develop the potential that you began to explore. You can improve your gifts and skills or strengthen the scab over the wounds. The Map leads you to continue your evolutionary learning through the cycles as a parent. You can heal old wounds and develop new ways that are more aligned with your values for this new opportunity of expression. You can become a leader, developing your skills and gifts for a higher purpose. You can choose to parent yourself, nurturing and developing your skills with the integration of the Elements. You will take into consideration the voice of your needs (Earth), the voice of your emotions and intuition (Water), the voice of your feelings (Fire), the voice of your mind (Air), with a positive intention (Ether). It is a continuous lifelong journey.

Foot Analysis, based on the Grinberg Method™

Through the reading of the feet, we can determine the basic trilogy for the personal growth process:

Your Actual Potential: This includes your behavioral patterns and any vicious cycles in which you find yourself entrapped.

The History of Mask Formation: Masks can be the bridge between then and now or the bridge between your mission and what you are doing now.

The Basic Potential: This is from your talents to your natural path, to access a space of contentment in the present.

In the DHARMI Map, I take into consideration the basic trilogy, which are reflected in the following ways:

Your reality of the moment, your illusion and the gap or connection between them.

Your daily actions, your higher purpose and whether you have either a space or bridge between them.

Your actual potential, your full potential and whether they are intertwined or distanced.

Your experiences, your integration or wisdom and the link in between them.

Your physical manifestation, your dreams and the gulf in between them.

The purpose of the Map is to clarify the path, the liaison in between the trilogy. The space in between them is the path of the heart. The relationship between them can improve from a space of acceptance and compassion. This supports us to deal with the duality we live in, where illusion and reality get closer and closer.

The Elements and Holistic Foot Analysis

When I became a Holistic Foot Reflexologist, after studying with Avi Grinberg in the early 1990's, I learned many things. The process gave me a very strong foundation and understanding of holistic therapies and bodywork, laying the groundwork for my future consulting work.

In that work, from a holistic perspective, I examine the connections between an individual's physical reactions, emotional responses and mental beliefs, as well as the circumstances that trigger or connect with his or her masks and behavioral patterns. These patterns are developed through experiences, and define a person's sense of identity or personality. When our reactions are repetitive, our cells and intelligence memory are programmed in a limited way. Though we are everything, we believe ourselves to be something much smaller... sometimes even insignificant.

Did You Know that Your Footprints Reveal Your Life's Path?

Our feet reflect the way we walk through life. References to the importance of the feet can be found in art, scripture, and sacred traditions around the world, from ancient Egyptian mythology to Christianity through Buddhism and Hinduism. Science and therapeutics also recognize the feet and reflexology, as a major pathway to healing and self-discovery.

Because the reflex points on our feet link into our body's meridians and nervous systems, they directly affect all areas of our body and being. Our footprints also contain a map of our life. Physical health, emotional memory, behavioral patterns and personal potentials are all reflected on our feet. The lines, callouses, swollen areas, tensions, and colors may be analyzed to see how past experiences are still affecting our energy levels and behavior at this time. Learning how to interpret those signs on the feet, considering the Elements, opens a door to greater awareness of ourselves and others. Some of the lines can be activating an Element or pointing to another. A callous can be an excess of Earth in a specific area of the foot, highlighting the imbalance of the person. For example, if a person has hard callouses on the balls of her feet, she will be feeling pressure on her chest. This reflects tightness in the thoracic area and upper back. In a holistic perspective, it represents the heavy responsibilities that weigh on her, limiting the expression of her feelings and thwarting her desires. She will prioritize obligations, holding back and procrastinating about fulfilling her own dreams.

If a person has hard, callused outer edges of both big toes, she will feel tightness in her jaw and back of her head, perhaps exacerbated by clenching her jaw. It reflects that every expression will be weighed and found important. For this person, it is hard to release and find room for lightness and breath.

We put pressure on areas of our feet in specific ways, as a response mechanism. It is a form of expression that affects our inner balance, as well as affects the moods and emotions of those around us. We leave a print on our path that reflects our perspective and our approach to life itself. Other peoples' paths and the way they walk that path influence us. We also influence others from the way we walk the journey.

Foot reflexology has been practiced for thousands of years and could even be considered one of the cornerstones of civilization, so widespread has been its use throughout history. The Ancients knew that our feet and their prints encapsulate and reflect our overall being. They embody our origins, our bodily and psychological forms, and our abilities. Additionally, the reflex points on our feet are connected to the nervous system so therefore to all aspects of our metabolism.

In reflexology analysis, the lines, callosity, swollen area, tensions, colors, and all other aspects of foot shape, form and texture are taken into consideration. We are provided with a foundation for observing how past experiences (behavioral patterns) are still influencing our present experience and energy level.

We live in a time where our attention and energy is mainly driven by the mind and we are most often engaged in seeking answers through research, trying to meet external goals or even embarking on spiritual quests. The connection to our feet—our very roots—allows us to ground ourselves, find a space of integrity and balance our energy. Yet all is in the here and now, on each step on our journey. Our past, our future, all is here with us. It is for us to choose our intention, our way, our rhythm and our direction. Each step that we make can become clearer. We become wiser as we walk. The more we learn from our life experiences, the clearer becomes our path. We get to know and accept who we are, our gifts and purpose as we walk and explore.

All is interconnected—our organs, our history and patterns, and our physical, emotional and mental health. Our perspective on life, the actions we take, as well as our ingrained response mechanisms all have an effect on every part of us. Our nervous system, how it handles stress, how our physical health is affected, will show in the state of our physical health. But, even more importantly, all the above will affect our fellow humans, too, as we are all part of one energy source. We all touch the same earth, leaving our imprint and own influence on our journey.

Holistic Foot Analysis and the Elements

AIR is represented by the toes, which concerns skin, breath, your mind, thought patterns, and belief systems.

FIRE is represented by the balls of the feet that concern your muscles' movement and energy, as well as the actions you take.

WATER is represented by the underside of your foot's arch, which concerns your digestive system and emotional responses.

EARTH is represented by your heel, which concerns your hips and immune system, the material plane and manifestation.

ETHER is represented by the entirety of the foot, which concerns the vital energy, the magnetism that brings life in all other aspects.

Exploring the Flow Through the Elements

Through the feet, we can observe the flow and relationship between the Elements, from inspiration to manifestation, as we have presented them in previous chapters. The expression of the Elements in our everyday life is a reflection of the way to we walk and express ourselves. All this is reflected by our own footprint.

We receive an inspiration, idea, or vision from the etheric level. This may come from a dream, from something we see, from a person we encounter or from an actual experience or intuitive feeling.

Our thought process is where we catch the dream with our mind. We enter into this process of the mind through analysis of the toes. How open is the mind to receiving new ideas? How developed is the ability to visualize? Observing the size of the toes, their flexibility and any specific signs helps clarify the way the person reflects and shows her perspective. We can learn how a person observes the world around her and how she processes ideas. The direction, length, and color of the toes gives us clues to all this. The Air Element is reflected in the toes.

The ball of the foot gives us insight on a person's motivation and ability to bring an idea to life, to take proactive steps to manifest something. This is the Fire Element.

How is the person's self-esteem? Are their feelings easily hurt? All this is reflected by the ball of the foot. Is it warm and strong? Or is it empty or repressed?

This may explain why so many women wear high heels, putting so much pressure on the balls of their feet and compressing the nerves of their toes. Such footwear can cover their own well-being and lack of self-esteem, mask their real image and substitute a vision of who they would like to be, and help them project a different image. The texture and strength in the area of the ball of the foot shows a person's self-esteem, and the direction in which the person is leading his or her actions and feelings.

If there were an excess of Earth in the Fire, the person would be busy with obligations, aspects that are related to money and family; working hard to try fulfill expectations that don't always take into consideration their feelings or true inspirations. If there is an excess of Air in that area of the foot, the person is easily distracted. This person will always look for reaffirmation of their potential action. They may have a lack of self-esteem, shutting down their feelings. They are intellectually driven. If there is an excess of Water, he or she will be influenced strongly by their surroundings and will need lots of emotional support and approval. The person will be very emotionally driven.

When the manifestation actually expresses itself, the element of Fire is doing it work. We can see the expression visually and quite clearly, as it is a form of outward communication.

What are the questions, fears or conclusions that may cause resistance to new ideas? The consideration of how one's personal energy flows in harmony or is stymied and mired down may be the cause. The emotional realm is what opens acceptance of new ideas or closes us off to them.

The area of the foot in between the ball of the foot and the heel is generally soft and pale. Are there many lines? These may express worries or a strong emotional influence. *Are the emotions repressed or fully expressed? How does the person channel his or her emotions?*

It is a space to observe the flow and honor clear emotional values and boundaries. If there are many lines in the water area of the foot, the person may have much interference and allow lots of interruptions in their flow. If that area is dry, it may be difficult for them to respect their own emotional space. They could be easily emotionally drained and may give way and fold, rather than stand up for their own values. A lack of support and their own sensitivity may stymie their decision-making ability.

The Water Element allows for integration of creativity, wisdom and flow, making room for the emotional aspect of the person to actually help their creativity to come into flower. Is the person in harmony with the environment and the community? Is the person listening to too many voices or are they attentive to their own intuition? Too much emotional support can overwhelm a person's creativity—just as in the old saying, "Too many cooks spoil the broth."

Other people may discover they have too much of the Fire Element within, causing scattered concentration and sometimes hyperactivity. Grounding can be the foundation for materialization. It can help to create the finances, structure, materials and space required for one's personal vision to manifest. The heel of the foot will determine if there is any resistance, unrealized in the flow of manifestation.

    I had an interesting experience with two people. One of them had a heel that was very dry and rough, while the other one had a soft and pliable heel. A person with healthy heels has a strong base and foundation, with abundant resources. Conversely, the one with the soft and pliable heels was coming from emotional attachments, more than they needed in fact for their personal evolution. The one with the dry heel had barely enough to survive, only just making their bills at month's end. Would that the one with more than he needed be willing to share with the one who had too little. Balance could have been achieved in both their lives. It didn't happen. These two never met. Each of them had their own learning experiences, their own paths to walk.

    It takes courage and compassion to accept that we must each walk our own path. Growing from our own root and Earth is all we can do. We are here to fulfill our own potential. It is only by following and expressing our potential that we can manifest our purpose. This later unfolds as we proceed on our journey. Walking through life is like a pilgrimage, unveiling wisdom, knowledge, and clarity, step-by-step. We can provide support to others only from a space of well-being and fulfillment.

    We cannot give water if our own glass is empty.

    Whenever I go to the ocean or any natural area, I collect trash that has been left behind by other people. One morning, with some friends, we collected seven big bags of trash. It was all cans of sodas or alcohol. Both of these substances are very unhealthy for people. How can we expect someone to be sensitive to their environment if they are not sensitive to their own well-being? People who are sensitive to their well-being, health and balance are more likely to choose water to drink and, even then, bringing refillable water bottles with them. You can choose to walk your path with health and mindfulness or disregard the lessons that are right in front of you.

I lived for two years in the south of Chile, on a mountain in the Andes near Argentina. Every few weeks, I traveled to San Martin de los Andes, a beautiful village in the Lake Region. One woman, who participated in the seminars I was teaching at that time, had a bunion on her foot. She was considering the option to have an operation. Though once she understood that the bunion meant she was exerting pressure on her heart, she chose to first explore another option by working on her life. She examined the pattern and approach in her relationships through the way she was walking. When she began to shift her body posture, building up her self-esteem day-by-day through mindfulness, she began to express herself from a space of self-confidence and acted accordingly to her feelings. After three months, she began to notice a very clear difference in her own life and in her feet. Some insightful shifts had happened. After six months, her foot was not bothering her anymore and she could walk with more ease.

The way we relate and express the Elements in our lives is reflected on our feet. We can affect their alignment and find more balance through external actions, changes of orientation, better perspective or by engaging in some healing work. All the approaches mentioned in this section complement each other. When we access a specific aspect using many of these external and internal experiences, the process of self or professional development will happen with harmony, mindfulness and integrity.

The Elements can be affected through foot reflexology, but also through meditation, dance, mindfulness and mandala making. The most important is to have a clear intention, clarify the Map and bring mindfulness into our form of expression.

Our life's path is reflected on our footprint and the way we walk is significant.

The way we channel our anger is reflected in the way we walk. We will press on specific areas of the feet. If we take our stand or if we lose control, when we feel that emotion, we will position our feet differently on the Earth. Our rhythm is different, the pressure on the feet is different and the influence on our life will be different. We affect ourselves and others around us on our way.

The Elements for Dance and Self-Expression

Evolution happens one step at a time. All of the processes in life happen step-by-step. What is your walking pattern? Your rhythm? Your direction? Forward? Backward? With ease? Struggling? Often turning around? With determination?

Sometimes we skip a step or we move with fear. At some moments, our hearts lead. At others, our fearful ego takes control. But we can help heal ourselves.

Dance is an insightful and healing form of expression, which can be done with the integration of the Elements.

I taught dance therapy and held moon circles for women during a few years in South, Central and North America and Europe. It was a very healing time for me and all the women I shared with on the path. I later organized workshops and classes for a women's shelter in Miami. It was a series of classes in which I integrated meditation, expression, dance and mandalas for healing and to empower women.

The response of the women has been remarkable. Class after class, they were finding more balance and a sense of empowerment. Most of the women in the shelter have been abused since early childhood. Whether it was psychological, emotional or physical abuse, they all found healing through self-expression, while balancing the Elements and channeling their creative energy with positive intention.

When I was teaching in a yoga studio in Montreux, a beautiful location in Switzerland, a man asked me why I didn't offer such a program for men. They also have to express themselves, they declared. So I developed a program that integrated the Five Elements through movement, channeling and expressing intention and included men in the finished program. Such work offered a profound process of healing, clearing, and empowerment for both sexes.

Dance provides the tools to help you connect with your heart and your personal dharma so you can free your energy and dance the dance of life with purpose and intention. As you connect with the energies of all Creation—movement, rhythm, and vision— you are taught to open the veil to the Divine Essence, health, well-being, and living life with grace and confidence.

Dance is the essence of freedom. Freedom has been interpreted in many ways. When I speak about freedom, I refer to the connection to your true essence and the realization of your life's purpose. In other words, living in dharma.

Freedom is a powerful sensation that reflects the ownership and acceptance of the responsibility of being you—the you that shines to its full potential, in connection to your heart, core values and intentions. Such freedom will bring your life into alignment with the principles in life's creation. That is a constant space of alertness and awakenings. Freedom is a powerful place to inhabit.

I have met many people who didn't know how to live free of conditions, expectations, and attachments. Sometimes they felt lost, disconnected, and struck out with no direction. They were rootless without intention or points of reference. Sometimes the fear of loss brought them back to unhelpful attachments. Sometimes they denied fundamental principles and acted out of alignment.

To experience freedom in our human experience, it requires a clear intention (Ether), organization and prosperity (Earth), emotional values and healthy relationships (Water), self-esteem and motivation (Fire) as well as clarity and direction (Air).

We use the dance and forms of expression of the Elements channeling them through the Five Bodies (the physical body, the emotional and digestive directly linked to the enteric nervous system, the energetic and self-esteem linked to the muscular system, the mental and breath directly linked with the cerebral nervous system and the spiritual body) to create that bridge between our inner being, our intention, our surroundings, loved ones, and environment. It is a way to relate, to communicate, to bond in all aspects and forms, from our heart center.

Expression through the Five Elements proves to be an experience of liberation with principles, values, connection and direction. We focus on our intention, release stress and allow the expression through our whole being.

Freedom can be experienced with discipline, purpose and intention. The foundation of freedom is a connection to your heart, values and life's principles. A moment of disconnection may lead you away from your freedom, from your heart. It could also be a space of ignorance, unconsciousness, and distraction. Freedom is a sacred space of enlightenment.

Freedom is a continuous, connected dance, which can expand and elevate your vibration and the vibration of others around you. You tune into the music and rhythm of your intention, creating those invisible strings and connections with others who tune in a similar wavelength, intention and mission on their life's path.

Traveling through many cultures, I observed and experienced rituals, which were performed with sacred dance. All forms of expression, in the dance from mudras, (a movement of the hand), the direction of a dancer's head, their costume and makeup, the placement of their foot and the times at which they take a breath, all have intention and meaning. The whole body is a form of expression, which influences our environment with a specific vibration. We affect our surrounding in the way we move, in the way we look at others, in the way we walk. How many actions and movements are now unconscious, done by habit, not by conscious intention? The response around us is affected by our own perspective and expression.

We can substitute one mirror after another. Our reflection won't change until we change our own form of expression, our own perspective and ways to be.

When you experience the dance passing through all Five Bodies (Elements channeled through your whole being with intention), there is a clear, tantric and pure experience in freedom. There are no shortcuts to reach freedom. It is a defined, sacred path unique for everyone. Your own rhythm and your own movement give you a sense of uniqueness and oneness simultaneously.

This dance includes music, rhythms and movements that invite the participant to experience the Elements in their own body's expression. This dance and form of expression releases tensions and opens the flow of creativity.

The process begins with creating a time and space to observe in what directions are your thoughts running? How do you feel? What is your mindset? Becoming still enough to recognize your position and expectations, while observing within you and what is around you.

Sounds of wind, wind instruments, lead you to tune in with the Air. The music awakens your senses, allow you to listen to the rhythm within and to the rhythm around you. Recognize if there is any resistance.

Bringing awareness to your breath and thoughts which cross your mind, clearing the mind and thus the body and clarifying your space will all help. Your mind is fully active and constantly thinking. What is your relationship with your thoughts? Observe, breathe, detach and clarify. The lightness of the Air can become heavy when it is overwhelmed by emotions, preconceptions or judgments. Take some time to lighten up.

The freshness of the wind gives space for the inspiration and Fire brings it into movement, allows its expression.

The shift of the music from the Air to the Fire invites the dancers to bring more feelings into their expression using the rhythm of the heart, tuning in with your own Fire. Observe your feelings. Are they repressed? How can you light up your Fire? Which movements and forms can open the access to your heart's expression? Let go of resistance and give space for movement, for nurturing, warmth and uplifting energy. When you learn to access your Fire Element, and express it consciously during the dance, you will have more tools with which to express yourself. You will find your balance and a healthy sense of self-esteem and flexibility will become evident in your communication.

The music will then invite you to move into the Water, a space of flow and emotions.

When you pass through those first layers of such resistance, you can access the emotional realm, observing your relationship with your emotions. Are there fears? Frustrations? Excitements? Can you surrender to your emotions? Release attachments and open the flow for more ease, harmony and transparency? Clearing the Water brings a sense of care and nurturing.

Then we enter in the drum of the Earth. This rhythm gives you space to settle and to ground yourself.

Feel the Earth below you. Listen to the rhythm of the drum. It is a subtle, yet profound, experience. The Earth is a heavy Element, grounding you. It's time to clear your base and heal your roots. In this stage of the dance, you heal and nurture a healthy ground. That foundation is fertile and welcomes the seed you want to plant. The connection with the Earth Element strengthens a sense of grounded ownership and solid foundation. With such increased security, you are better able to shoulder your own responsibility. You will learn to respect your space and values and those of others ones around you. You feel more self-contained and assertive in your expression when needed.

A sacred dharmic moment, planting the seed of your intention, is profound and experienced within, accessing stillness as you did in the womb, where you rested and nested.

You can stay there if it is evening time. You will ascend through the Elements with the Element of Ether, via singing bowl or gong sounds. It is a time of integration, surrender and assimilation.

If you prefer to begin from the roots, from the Earth and move up through the different rhythms and forms of expression towards the Water, Fire, Air, and Ether, this is perfectly fine as well.

Feel the heart of the Earth, the drum within, the drum surrounding you getting stronger and stronger. It invites you to change, like a seed transforming into a plant, breaking through the old and giving birth to the new. Feeling the Earth below your feet is a way to remind yourself of this temporary human experience we live in. Feel your body, the primitive part of you. Let the sexual energy flow and express itself. Be rooted and allow space for your needs to be taken care of.

With the flowing movement and rhythms of Water, you nurture and care for that new manifestation. This is a time for acceptance, flowing with gentle moves, exploring new sensations and forms of expression. Emulate the circles of the dance. Allow grace to emerge and emotions to be released. Surf the waves with intention and navigate and channel your emotions with creativity, sensibility and intuition.

A new you is awakening. Visualize and express your intention in your movements. Let it shine and give it space for self-expression. Direct your flame with warmth and charisma. Express your Fire with confidence. Dance with character, expressing your gifts, your intention and your authentic self fully.

Stand tall and own this new role. Visualize it and feel it, reflecting fully this intention in your movement, in your breath, in your full expression. The Air brings lightness. It gives you space and the wings to fly and to imagine. Feel the delightful sense of release, detachment and freedom.

Take a moment to surrender to the Ether, honoring a moment for integration, for surrender to Bliss.

The rhythms and movement supports you to awaken and balance your Five Elements, balancing your energy, empowering them and clearing the relationship between them. This cycle opens the flow in your creativity. You will now have the power to manifest inspirations, visions and intentions within the material world.

The steps leading you through the Elements allow you to discover and access the frequency, quality, rhythm and potential of each of them. The more familiar you become with those different forces, the better you can manage life's situations.

The Dance helps clear patterns in our body language and self-expression. It provides more awareness in our communication and interactions through the day.

When Rafael was first introduced to the Dance of the Elements, he had his feet so grounded, he couldn't move them. They stayed solid and stuck, as if he had no freedom to move them. He could move his upper body freely and, open his mind and expression in other

Elements. Yet, the Earth was now heavy and the feeling overwhelmed him. He began to do little steps, very unsecure and rigid.

In the next few days, he began to notice aspects in his life beginning to move. His foundation was moving. At his next DHARMI consultation, he found more flexibility in his Earth. He noticed that he had more space to move and felt a sense of abundance that he hadn't experienced previously.

In the next few months, his whole life underwent a big shift. Through our work together, he felt profound emotions and release. He was finding more clarity. As he built up more self-confidence, he noticed that he was able to love more unconditionally and with less expectation.

He relocated with his family to another country, where they found much more harmony, ease, and a better education for their children. He was more at peace with his values and could express his creativity freely in that new location. He pulled his feet out of the muck and set them on a new path.

As the path continues to unveil wonders, we are still in communication regularly, clarifying intention and nurturing his true connection.

The Five Elements in Meditation

Meditation refers to a practice in which we train our mind to reach a state of stillness, consciousness and bliss.

The meditation practice is inspiring and allows you to enter in a blissful state of being. It is beautiful to share quality time, a moment that is so nurturing, healing and uplifting.

The **DHARMI Meditations** lead you through a profound practice and awakening in holistic way. Dance is an active meditation. Qigong & Yoga are also forms of active meditation. The Vortex of Energy Meditation is another pathway in the Map, which supports you to align the Seven Tonalities with the resonance of your intention. It is a profound journey that I present in the book Resonance on the Journey.

When I was 15 years old, I spent hours in my bed, trying to levitate, imagining myself liberated from this physical and material realm. I couldn't speak with my family or friends about it, as it was too strange for them to even imagine. I was focusing on some words, colors and visions, which I read about in books that I found. It was giving me peace and enough space to have a sense of freedom and clarity. It gave me some distance from all the family pressure and confusion that I was experiencing at that time.

I practiced the 10 day Vipasana meditation at the age of 20, while most of my friends where pursuing a more traditional life's path. They were focusing on building up relationships, trying to find the right job or the right person with whom to create a family.

My quest has been constantly exploring the inner labyrinth, which opens doors above time and space, towards other dimensions. I did vision quests with shamans, five years in a row, and received many answers. I was constantly evolving on my journey. I had the opportunity to practice transcendental meditation, Buddhist meditations, shamanism, mantras, prayers, ceremonies and sacred dances. I found a Map that was supporting me to integrate those practices, with grace, into my life.

I noticed that an intense practice of meditation, if not done with intention and clear direction, could cause a sense of disconnection with my everyday life and my life as an incarnated being. In some situations, I felt a stress or resistance between the meditation, the inner journey, and the manifestation into my daily life. I had to journal to make sure I could connect the two—the plane on which I reached through meditation and the daily life to which I returned when my meditation was done.

Many times, people who were using meditations had difficulty integrating them, and finding a bridge to their everyday life. Therefore the meditations didn't invite harmony into their relationships, prosperity in their work life, or purpose and joy to their roles as members of society.

With the meditations leading through the Map, we focus on the integration of the intention in a holistic way, to allow a space for the embodiment. This reminds us that we are spiritual beings having a human experience. We honor all aspects in our embodiment, with the chaos, flow, and movements that are part of our life's experience. When we enter into that meditation, we bring awareness in our thought process, our actions and emotions. We learn to channel them with more clarity, compassion, and intention.

This approach is a very good complement with other forms of meditation, as it supports the process of integration in our culture, communication, relationships and the material realm we live in.

Meditation helps to manage stress, release attachments and access a space of peace, clarity and bliss.

But meditation, focus and visualization require training, like a muscle. The more we practice compassion, the more natural it becomes to be compassionate towards our environment, our loved ones and ourselves.

The more we focus our mind with clarity, liberating ourselves from distractions or ego, the more natural it becomes to honor our intention and follow our path.

One of the main practices is to bring awareness to your state of being in the moment and to clarify an intention for your practice. This meditation is with a visualization and contemplation of the Five Elements, bringing clarity of your point of reference in the here and now.

I have practiced meditation daily for more than 20 years, and noticed subtle differences in my way of being every time I enter into the practice. It is as if I am gauging my inner barometer, in order to guide my intention, attention, and actions with clarity through the day.

A practice is focused on the Cycle through the Elements. This allows you to honor a healthy relationship between the Five Elements. It supports the possibility of channeling energy with clarity and intention. If you notice that one of the Elements is agitated or seems drained, you will guide more energy into that space to allow a release and flow or to energize and strengthen a space of weakness.

When we practice meditation, we create a distance from those adverse conditions and take responsibility of our actions, emotions, feelings, and thoughts. Meditation aims to reach a space of stillness, emptiness and pure connection to the source, to your true essence.

Passive meditation can be done in a standing posture, seated or laying down. Meditation can be guided through specific visualizations, breathing practices, or contemplation. There are many different levels of meditations. Here I share with you the one that brings awareness into the Elements and balance into your life.

Meditation awakens your potential of alignment, the connection to your intentions, values and higher purpose. It integrates within your reality to incarnate and manifests in the physical and material world.

The flow of energy is vital in life's creation. Passing through and clearing the different levels of fundamental Energies within you allows you to access the Five Bodies: mental (*Air*), energetic (*Fire*), emotional (*Water*), physical (*Earth*), spiritual (*Ether*).

This practice allows the integration and consciousness of your whole being in a holistic way through your thoughts, actions, emotions, relationships, physical manifestations and spiritual energies.

The rhythms, words, and guidance will support you to free your creative potential, empowering the energies/Elements in the process, and allowing the transition from one to the other energy/Element. This practice empowers manifestation of inspirations, vision, or insights within the material world. It can be focused on an inner insightful experience, as well as an external project and creation that you visualize.

Sit comfortably in a chair or on a pillow, in a peaceful place where you know that you won't be distracted. It would be better if you were seated with the spine long, without your back being supported by external props, unless you need to have support at the beginning of your practice, or if you have a specific health reason.

Make sure not to be distracted by the external environment for the next 15-45 minutes. Shut off your phone. If you live with someone, clarify that you will need to be undisturbed for your set amount of time. Don't have a TV or computer on around you. You can follow one of the guided meditations on iTunes, or if you like to practice on your own, you can use smooth music or sounds for meditation such as gongs, singing bowls or nature sounds, making sure that the sounds will be appropriate and support your practice and concentration.

Write down on a piece of paper the specific thoughts (*shopping list, calls you have to make, worries, etc.*) to clear from your mind. This way you can come back to those thoughts after the meditation and not interrupt your time of introspection and connection. This is a way to begin the clarification of your mind. Take a moment to observe where you are at this moment. It is a time of contemplation without judgment.

I invite you to look around, observe what surrounds you and bring mindfulness in the smells, the tastes, the rhythm, and the temperature of the surrounding area. Are there any reactions or any sensations that are triggered?

What is the temperature of the air when it is coming into your lungs? What is the temperature of the air when it comes out of your body? Is your inhalation longer or shorter than your exhalation?

Look at your thought process as if you were looking at the sky. Observe if there are clouds, some to which you are attaching to, some that you can detach from and just contemplate. How is your sky and perspective at this time? Sometimes you have judgments, preconceptions or expectations. Sometimes you may notice a duality between the imagination and what you really see, between the illusion and the reality.

Observe and contemplate that beautiful sky, that mind and all its movement, breathe as though you moving the wind to direct the clouds, to welcome the thoughts with acceptance and compassion. *Who are you behind the thoughts?*

You can deepen your experience by bringing awareness of your feelings at this time and the rhythm of your heart. This drum is in constant movement, so strong, so powerful, yet so sensitive and vulnerable. This big heart is moving in the core of your chest. It is moved by your breath and lungs. It also supports the movement of your breath and lungs. The relationship between the Air and the Fire, the thoughts and the feelings, is direct and instant. Just one thought can hurt or heal your heart. Take a moment to nurture your heart, to feel your heart beat within your chest. Feel the rhythm of the heart as the walking, trotting or galloping of the horse. Sometimes it may want to gallop like a wild horse. Can you ride it with grace, strength, love and care, nurturing the relationship with your heart? The more we try to control, judge or dominate our feelings, the more our horse suffers. *Can you guide, lead and ride it with respect and intention?* This will improve that wonderful dance in between the Elements.

You can then dive deeper into the Water. Those emotions that are in movement, changing and mysterious, are just like our relationships. That Element is sometimes flowing, other times it dries out or become so cold that it freezes. *How does it feel in your stomach? Is it a sensation of flow, is it contained or is it completely loose or stuck?* Observe. Bring awareness to your belly and to your emotional state at this moment. There are no negative emotions. It is the way you interpret them, the way you channel them, what you do with and about them that can transform them into positive or negative. Can you accept your sensitivity and your intuition?

I suggest you to try to allow the expression of your creative spark, your inner child, with acceptance, clarity and direction. Diving deep in our inner ocean gives us the chance to clear repressed emotions, to explore and discover beautiful mysteries. Looking within can become a magical adventure, opening the flow within and all around you.

Then, you can ground yourself and observe the bed of the river or the bottom of the ocean as though it were the structure or foundation of your body. You can notice the stillness and solidity of your bones, accessing a profound layer of your physical body. Your base can feel quite primitive and heavy. Yet the deeper we root ourselves, the higher we can fly. Is there any taboo related to your sexuality or to your physical needs? When you sit still in this stable place, honoring your time, your own space, you can feel a profound sense of security, support and belonging.

From that place of awareness, what would be your main intention at this time? What is the key word left after you have achieved clarity? It can be peace, stillness, compassion, love, bliss, or any other that resonates with you at this time of your life.

You can come out of your meditative experience now, and engage your intention into your way of being through your day.

Another approach to meditation through the Elements requires you to ask yourself some questions and clarify your intention prior to beginning the meditation:

Psychologically: *Where are your thoughts? How is your breathing?*

Energetically: *How is your energy level? Do you feel the rhythm and strength of your heart beat—the pulse of life?*

Emotionally: *How do you feel at this time?*

Physically: *Is there any tension, pain or numbness in a specific area of your body?*

Clarify your intention: Write down what you seek. *Which of these do you long for: peace, alignment, love, connection, inner strength or clarity? Do you wish to respect your body, honor your feelings or intuition, or develop compassion?* Remember your intention clearly throughout your meditation.

In the next few steps you can focus and visualize on bringing that intention into the Five Elements.

Observe how your breath is when you tune into your intention. Bring consciousness to the breath and the rhythm. Breathe into your inspiration and clarification through the air. Imbue your intention with lightness. It is a place where you can empower and affirm your intention.

Try to feel your heart beat. Tune into your inner rhythm. Catch the idea and intention with your fire. Feel in your rhythm and active self the behavior and reflection of your new point of reference.

Feel the Water flow within your body. Allow the integration with harmony and connection to your inner child. Feel the emotions that are connected to your intention. Notice how you can channel your emotions with intention.

Connect with your bone structure. Feel your bones, the grounding, and visualize the foundation within the Earth Element. Allow the grounding and manifestation in a secure, confident and stable space.

Bring in Water to let it grow, with playfulness, sensitivity, and creativity. Feel the water flowing around the bones and muscles. Feel it pour into your veins and internal organs.

Feel the connection to the rhythm of your heart, to your inner rhythm. Allow it to appear with a spark of Fire and uplift the emotion. Connect to the personal way of expressing your intention and values.

Free the completion through the Air. Release with awareness to your breath, while connecting to the rhythm. Invite it in deeply to open your lungs. Give and receive, allowing the interaction between the inner and outer world and reality. Release and free the information and clearly reflect your intention.

Connect with all. Feel the light and a space of liberation, in pure connection. Allow the expansion of your vibration. You are fully in tune with your intention, you become one with it.

At the end of the meditation, take your time to look from within toward the outside. Return to where you are. Drink a glass of water. If some insights came during the practice, I suggest you to write them down in your journal.

Integration

During the day after the meditation, you may notice more synchronicities in your life. Learn to listen and be open to the responses that you may receive from your practice. Be open to possibilities. People have noticed that they felt more present, creative, confident and conscious in their life after this practice. Also, they are alert and ready to respond with authenticity, to the signs and possibilities that are aligned with their intention.

A daily practice of meditation leading through the Map supports a conscious evolution. It allows you to observe where are you today, how you feel, what is happening, and direct your attention, energy and actions with clear intention.

It reminds you where you are on your life's journey at this specific moment. When you develop more expertise in your practice and tune with awareness, alertness, and integrity, it will become like your inner guidance, astrology, tarot card, and statement for your day.

If you look at the sunset every day, you will notice that it is never exactly the same. If you are in a relationship, your own interpretation, your own feeling about that person will change depending of the experiences, thoughts and expectations that comes along. Sometimes we try to access an old feeling or perception that is not present anymore. It takes a lot of effort to attach to what is gone. It is stressful to try to resist changes.

We live in a constant evolution and meditation supports you to take in consideration those natural changes.

It is normal that there is change and you feel differently. We are creatures of habit, yet the more we attach to something, to someone, to a substance, the more we detach from our truth and core. Those attachments are ways to let go of our deepest responsibility. They are the source of karma and suffering.

If you learn to open your heart and feel profound sense of love in a relationship, you can choose to welcome and build up that sense of love. This is a gift that you receive. But it doesn't mean that you have to stay attached to the other person. You can welcome the gift, share from a space of love and clarity and honor the path of both of you. Whether your paths continue together, whether your paths become more distant, the love can still remain.

We can focus on healthy habits, such as an honorable meditation practice. This habit will remind you to be flexible and to lead your actions with acceptance and compassion.

It is humbling to practice meditation, to honor our relationships and the divine flow of evolution. While it can be humbling to give in to our truth, the power of love is much healthier than choosing to control and attach to expectations.

Reality is what you choose to believe in. You have the freedom to choose your reality, to choose what you like to believe in. One shift of perspective can change your whole life's experience.

Those meditation practices support you to navigate through life's transitions.

Meditation helps to gain distance from impulsive responses or actions. It is a way to be mindful of our thought process, of our emotions, and to give them space to settle, to clarify. It teaches us to access our responsibility instead of being reactive to life's circumstances, fears and triggers.

When we bring mindfulness through meditation in the Five Elements, we awaken more aptitudes and find a liaison between our actions, thoughts, emotions, and manifestations. It is a way to bring the pieces of the puzzle together, from our center.

Integrating the Elements in Healing Through Touch

Balancing the Five Bodies helps us enter a profound process of integration and healing. When we notice an imbalance in a specific Element, they usually reflect in the Five Bodies.

The Earth is the immune system, the bone structure, hips, legs, and grounded sensation of your body. The touch of the Earth is heavy, grounded and slow. It gives a sense of support to the foundation.

The Water is reflected in the digestive system and the distribution of fat and fluid through the body. It also reflects the health of the internal organs in general, as well as the enteric nervous system. The touch of the Water is fluid, moving constantly, gently nurturing and comforting. It gives a chance to release emotions and open the flow.

The Fire is mainly reflected through the muscles and movement, as well as heart rate and biorhythm. The touch of the Fire is more active and directed mainly in the muscle mass, observing if there are any points of muscle tightness, resistance, or lack of energy.

The Air is in the breath, cerebral nervous system and skin. The Air is directly connected to the senses, even as all the senses are interconnected to all the Elements. The touch of the Air is light. It adapts its rhythm and direction in alignment with the intention. It brings lightness. It is a stress reliever.

The Ether is in the electromagnetic field, the vital energy that connects it all. The touch is in the magnetic field.

After a clear evaluation of the person's Elements and current states, the session will be driven towards one Element or a combination, following a specific purpose.

Elements in Mandala Design for Healing and Balance

The mandalas are symbols that reflect specific purpose and vibration in an energetic level, which are aligned with an intention and direction. They have been used in different traditions. They symbolize life's principles and affect those who view them in specific ways.

We can use them to awaken our creativity, for empowerment or for visualization. It helps clarify some aspects in a process of development for balance and integration.

A mandala is the reflection of the universe, its source and expansion. It can be interpreted as the embryo and the womb, as the source and the field containing manifestation and creation.

A mandala can be symbolized by a flower, a garden, an eye, the sun, a face, a tree or the planet itself. The word mandala comes from spiritual and ritual symbols in Hinduism and Buddhism, though it is now also used in the Western approach to psychology as practiced by Carl Jung and his followers.

A mandala honors the fact that all creation is a projection coming from the innermost center, as embodied in a circle. Shapes can vary in their representation. However, they usually reflect balance, creation and the Four Gates or directions.

The creation and visualization of a mandala helps to focus attention towards specific purposes and intentions. It allows the relief of stress or trauma. It does liberate us from attachments—opening the door to other dimensions.

The basic form of most mandalas is a square, with Four Gates containing a circle with a center point. Sometimes the gates are in the general shape of a 'T'. Most of the time, they exhibit radial balance. I have been surprised to see these symbols in so many gardens and parks. The rose garden at the Jimmy Carter Museum in Atlanta is designed in a shape of a mandala. Most of the plazas in the villages and cities throughout South America have a similar shape.

In various spiritual traditions, a mandala is used as a spiritual teaching tool, to focus and establish a sacred space and as an aid to meditation, healing and trance. Mandala is now a generic term for any plan, chart or pattern that represents the cosmos metaphysically or symbolically.

Creating a mandala based on the Five Elements can support your balance and awaken your creative energy. Symbols, colors, shapes, and even words may be used to clarify the interaction and the alignment in between the Earth, Water, Fire, Air and Ether Elements.

This Map used to present an idea, vision or concept and gives the opportunity to realize if there are misalignments. If one of the Elements is dominating the others, the Map helps point out a better way to balance them for a more integrative healing, understanding or development.

Mandalas support the healing and visualization, honoring a representation of a microcosm of the universe from the human perspective. They are symbols that reflect a vision and vibration in an energetic field which are aligned with a specific intention, purpose, and direction. They have been used in different traditions, symbolize life's principles, and affect those who see or use them in specific ways.

When we consider the expression and position for the Elements in the artistic creation, it brings clarity and gives us a chance to see if there are imbalances in the process. Also, it allows us to observe the interrelationship between each aspect of the personal life or business. The integration of a mandala supports the balance between the creative aspect and the linear rational aspect of a project. It allows the opening and clarification of some dimensions of a project that are not perceivable in a linear process of thought and functionality.

This way of expression opens the flow of your creative energy and for the manifestation of inspiration within the material realm.

A licensed DHARMI Holistic Consultant developed his gift in painting through creation of mandalas. He uses the Five Elements in his process, from the vision to the manifestation of his work. He follows and brings the Elements to all his creation and visualization, to create with integrity and a sense of wholeness in all fundamental aspects.

He wrote,

"*I appreciate the review of the Elements and to see how they can be explained simply and clearly. Today I honor the Elements as my paintbrush dances across my canvas.*

The Air brings me clarity and focus.

The Fire reflects my intention in each brushstroke.

The Water cleanses the colors of the paintbrush.

The Earth celebrates and decorates the life of the canvas, which has offered herself to me for a new life.

The Ether supports me to integrate this space of pure love, enjoying myself in a positive and uplifting way."

—— G.G.

Finding oneself in front of a blank white page can be challenging. It is similar to when we notice that we have new doors opening on our path. We find ourselves entering into a new reality, a new chapter in our life.

Looking at the blank white page, you can take a moment to center yourself and clarify your mind. You can use the meditation mentioned previously to clarify your intention of the moment. I suggest you to use the same intention that you chose earlier through the meditation and imagine how this intention can be reflected in a mandala.

From that intention, you will choose a color that represents it the most, and draw a dot or a symbol in the center of your page. You will also define its space. This is the reflection of the Ether. You can make a dot in the center of your page while focusing on your intention. Remember to focus on your breath and your intention through the whole creative expression.

Imagine which color would reflect your intention, in each of the layers in the manifestation. You can use different colors, shapes, words, and create your own art piece.

Once the center and theme is clear, you can visualize and draw how you see this intention manifesting in the other Elements. How can this intention be contained and supported? How can this intention be reflected in the Water, allowing a space to bring the flow and emotional touch into it? How can you represent it in the Fire, visualizing the actions and ways of expression? How can you represent it in the Air, visualizing the thoughts or forms of reflection? I suggest you express yourself freely on your paper, using symbols, shapes, and colors with intention and direction. You can use your creativity, making a collage, using pencils, watercolors, or even using natural materials like stones, flowers, leaves or whatever is symbolic to you at this time.

You can organize the Elements on the cardinal points of your creation. Then, you will place four dots around this center, one for each Element. You can do four big petals, one for the Earth, one for the Water, one for the Fire and the last one for the Air. The center and the whole mandala itself is the reflection of the Ether.

You can also choose to organize the Elements from within the mandala's frame or use the Elements as though they were ripples in a pond. Both options will serve the purpose. Yet the combination of both can make it even clearer.

Once your mandala is completed, you can take a moment to integrate the result of your expression. You can observe it, meditate with it or share it.

An insightful journey that I suggest to people is to take a moment to write a list of all the colors, numbers, shapes, and symbols that they included in their creation. And then, write a story, intuitively, translating those into words. It has always been a very interesting and insightful way to realize more about oneself.

You are free to express yourself and can do it with intention and the proper tools to channel it clearly.

Creativity requires direction, technique, context and intention. To clarify your intention, you can use the tools that I provided earlier through a meditation. The context is the Elements on your journey. You can choose to focus on one of the specific themes mentioned previously in the book, such as well-being and lifestyle, relationships, leadership, mindfulness, process from inspiration to manifestation.

The technique is to use the shape of the mandala, which means the center point and all around being the Ether and the four Elements can have one cardinal point for each one of them.

Mandalas can be created individually, as well as in group, family or for an organizational project or vision.

Such a symbol can serve to clarify the intention, and how the gifts and visions of everyone on the team combine to create a bigger picture. The project, vision and mission are clearly set and the team members find the ways to complement each other's forces, skills and potentials for that purpose.

I have led seminars integrating the rational, linear aspect of holistic development, as well as the creative aspect, with the integration of mandalas for organizations and events. We used the expression of mandalas to set and clarify the goals and strengthen the teamwork, as well as to outline the steps necessary to bring them into manifestation.

It is a creation that supports the specific purpose for a group, organization or community, allowing a space for everyone to express themselves and find their space.

The mandalas are created with a specific intention and purpose for the group. Often this purpose is to better structure their organization and have integrity in the process of manifestation.

Once a mandala is completed, it can be used as a reminder and reflection of the intention of the group and community so they can keep it or have it photographed for perpetuity.

Sometimes the creation is given away, when it is created in nature or with recycled materials, as a reminder of the law of impermanence, to release expectations and stay in the present moment

The creation of a mandala for a group requires some time of introspection and clarification before setting it up. I take into consideration the theme and vision (Air), the motivation and purpose (Fire), the team and emotional space of everyone (Water), the framework and resources that are their disposal (Earth). The whole creation and project can be developed with intention and direction (Ether).

Once, I prepared a beautiful foundation and structure for a mandala that was going to travel with a man around the United States. His purpose was to connect the community and the people who he would meet on his travels, with peace and awareness. I created a foundation on a canvas and magnetized it with positive and focused visualization.

The day he began his travels, we organized a gathering in the town to see him off. People began to fill up spaces in the mandala with their own intention and energy. The next day, he took the mandala with him to another state. He traveled through many cities and took the mandala out each time he was holding a gathering. He invited the participants to add positive intentions via colored pebbles to this art piece. It grew as the community was growing, with a harmonious peaceful intention and a sense of connectedness between all those who participated and the beautiful mandala.

Many people who have created their mandalas with intention and clarity in their form of expression have noticed how much their path opened following their creation and how manifestation resulted. It is all about focus and creativity with integrity.

I have also integrated the Elements and the Map in my yoga practice and now teach DHARMI-YOGA®. It is a blissful journey of intention through asanas, bringing the philosophy of yoga and practice in all Five Elements, and one that I will write about in an upcoming book.

From our center we can create, form, shape and experience our intention. From within, we live the life from a point of reference that reflects a clear perspective. Our happiness or love doesn't only depend of what surrounds us. It is a state of being, an intention that we can integrate in all forms of our lives.

If we act from love, we experience love. If we direct our thoughts and channel our emotions with love, we can feel the love. If we receive love, yet we deny it or judge ourselves, we distance ourselves from it. The most beautiful is when the experience of love is within and all around us, and shared with bliss.

CONCLUSION

We all have our own gifts, talents and paths to walk. We meet each other and learn from each other. We complement each other.

When we are mindful of the constant evolution and movement in the Elements within and around us—it keeps us awake, alert and open to life.

We can choose to become wiser through our life's experience. We can unveil life's wonders when we open ourselves to such experiences.

We all have our strengths and our weaknesses. When we learn more about ourselves, we can better deal with our life and clarify our relationships with others around us.

It is in our hands to choose the direction of our perspective and life.

In all forms of expression, from our professional life, to our relationships; from our lifestyle to our mindfulness; from our leadership skills to our stress management; from our way of living to our health, we can find a representation, affect the balance, and gain an alignment of the Elements. We can use them for creativity, to serve an intention and higher purpose or we can suffer from their imbalance. The choice is up to you.

- DHARMA MAP -

GLOSSARY

Energy: In physics, energy is a property or object that can be transferred to other objects or converted into different forms, but cannot be created or destroyed. However, there are many other definitions of energy, such as thermal energy, radiant energy, electromagnetic, nuclear energy, etc.

In this book, I speak about five fundamental Energies aligned with the Five Elements. The physical and material energy is in direct relation with the Earth Element. The emotional energy is connected with the Water Element, while the intellectual energy is linked with the Air Element. The Fire Element is reflected in the energy of action and movement. And the spiritual electromagnetic energy is related with the Ether Element. They are all intertwined and support each other for balance and development in our life.

Holistic: This book considers a holistic perspective to health, well-being and personal and professional development. This means that it takes into consideration the integrity and the five Elements as a whole. All aspects are interconnected and complement each other.

Resonance: Resonance is the way a space or our body reflects a sound or frequency. When we balance and clarify the seven tonalities within us, our frequency is aligned with the intention we choose to tune in. It is a resonance that we reflect in our whole being, into our lives and affect our surroundings. I consider the seven tonalities within us being the voice of our heart, our spirit, our inheritance (ancestral DNA), our mind, our emotions, and our energetic and physical selves. When they are all in tune with a clear intention, we resonate and reflect that frequency within and all around us.

- DHARMA MAP -

APPENDIX
OTHER PATHWAYS ON THE MAP

The DHARMI MAP

The Map is based on three fundamental pathways:
The Cycle through the Elements

This cycle supports the flow of creativity and energy within and around you. It is about allowing balance and healthy relationships between yourself and life and the Five Elements (Air, Fire, Earth, Water and Ether).

The Vortex of Energy Meditation

This Meditation practice supports the alignment in the Five Elements (Air, Earth, Water, Fire and Ether) and the Seven Tonalities (the mind, the feelings/behaviors, the emotions, the physical, spiritual, ancestral and heart center/essence).

Forms to be studied and mastered include:
- Liberation and clearing
- Alignment and centering
- Expansion and manifestation
- Integration

The Cycle of Evolution:

This is a journey that invites you to reflect and clarify your point of reference at this time of your life. Through the process, you will have the possibility to heal, accept your reality and awaken new potential. It consists of Five Steps:

Step One: Clarifying a specific context or situations that may trigger stress at this time of your life.

Step Two: Focusing on identification of your reaction. What does this situation or person trigger in you? Observing your masks and your response mechanism in a holistic way.

Step Three: Connection to your heart center, clarification of your intention and centering.

Step Four: Clarification of a new perspective and role in a holistic way. Redefining your perspective, expression, approach, and ego.

Step Five: Integration within your life.

Entering the Cycle of Evolution

At the core of the MAP is a path called the *Cycle of Evolution*. It was inspired by my personal experiences, insights and research on rites of passage in different cultures. It is the collection of enlightening teachings, practices and guidance, which I have channeled in a clear methodology.

This Cycle leads us through specific steps to address situations in our lives with a new perspective. It is a holistic approach to stress awareness and management.

With a clear mind, body and soul, we enter a space of well-being and grace. We tune into our own heart center and we become more connected to the Source— the Ether, a higher vibration, the divine connection.

Many forms of therapy focus on the problem and its release. However, if we don't learn a new way to be and have not transcended the trauma, we are likely to continue repeating patterns. Awakening new potentials and accessing inner strength, clarity and compassion is the key that allows us to free ourselves from vicious cycles.

The *Cycle of Evolution* offers a holistic way to redirect emotional memory, intelligence memory and cell memory. It is a tool for renewal. Just as our cells renew daily, our perception can be updated with consciousness and intention. In the process, we can release old patterns on many levels, and create nurturing habits.

The steps through this cycle allow us to receive the wisdom from our experiences so that we can learn and grow from them. You may find yourself moving through life with greater wisdom, consciousness, purpose and abundance.

The Five Steps in the Cycle of Evolution

Each step is developed in the book *Cycle of Evolution*:

In *Step 1*, observe which situation, memory, expectation or relationship awakens a feeling of stress or triggers a reaction that takes you out of your heart center. This is the stress that seems to be coming from outer circumstances. If you notice many sources of stress, you can focus on the most important one at this time in your life.

Through *Step 2*, you clarify the primary cause of your stress. This is your reaction, or point of reference, which comes from the accumulation of emotional memories and past experiences. You will identify four components: a core belief, the sensations created by that belief and triggered by the situation, the emotional responsibilities and any behavioral patterns linked to the belief and situation.

Step 3 is the moment of transcendence and connection to your heart center, through acceptance, forgiveness and gratitude. Behind the mask waits a gift. There is a gift in any crisis. This Step is felt as a sensation, sometimes abstract, in which we re-encounter and access our inner guide or master. This experience can be subtle and powerful. In this state of being, we find inspiration and a key intention that liberates us from duality. We enter a space of awakening.

From this space of clarity and intention, we enter *Step 4*—embodiment. Drawing from our higher self, we express and align our vibration, sensations and thoughts. We consider the seven directions or tonalities (*North, South, East, West, Above, Below and Center*) and the Five Elements (*Earth, Water, Fire, Air and Ether*).

The last stage, *Step 5*, is the invitation to relate with our surroundings from a new perspective. Our way of looking at life's circumstances and opportunities can now come from a new expanded perspective and level of awareness. Friends, family and coworkers may notice a change. One day, someone said to someone else, who has awakened new potentials and moved on with intention and abundance, "*Why are you not staying like all of us, doing what is expected from us, responding to our conditioned environment and education? You look so liberated, alert and fulfilled.*" This person noticed that she had liberated herself from conditioning and duality at a very particular level, and could now relate to her family, career and life with freedom and grace.

Every step in the Cycle of Evolution is important. If we skip Step 3, we will continue our karmic path in duality, passing from reaction to reaction. If we skip

Step 4, we may have a feeling of well-being and peace, but won't have embodied this feeling integrally. If we stay in Step 1, we touch only the secondary aspect of our stress, blaming external conditions without healing the root or cause of it. If we forget Step 5, it will be difficult to communicate and relate with our loved ones and surroundings.

The first Step is to examine what is now affecting you and taking you out of your center. The second Step is to recognize the repetitive behaviors you want to change by focusing on physical reactions, emotional responses, mental beliefs and the circumstances related to those actions.

You will recognize the causes and roots of your habitual reactions through regression and bodily and physical manifestation. By moving beyond your reactions, you will discover and connect with hidden talents and gifts. Your power will be freed and clarified when you release limitations. As part of this empowering and conscious practice, you activate and manifest your intention by creating a new point of reference. You see life from a new perspective and access infinite possibilities.

It is a powerful, yet subtle process of evolution that allows you to learn and unveil your potential, become aware of repetitive patterns, duality, and allow for a harmonious, mindful and inspiring perspective on your path.

Vortex of Energy Meditation

The Vortex of Energy Meditation is one of the three pathways in the Map. It can be practiced independently, or integrated with the other two. It supports the alignment in the seven tonalities with a clear intention and resonance.

After 20 years of dedication, studies, and teachings in different modalities, such as meditation, dance-therapy, qigong, yoga and shamanism, I did a synthesis, combining some of the main Elements of those, to bring them into a simple, yet powerful, active meditation.

The purpose to practice this active meditation is to clear your magnetic field, align the Five Elements and Seven Tonalities.

The Seven Tonalities that are taken in consideration are the mind, the feelings and behaviors, the emotions, the physical, spiritual, ancestral (DNA, family tree), and heart center or essence.

When we clarify the relationship and balance those Seven Tonalities, we find a space of bliss. We align our resonance with a positive intention, which opens the path to new possibilities and synchronicities.

It is an active meditation that reminds the practitioners to move, clear and balance their inner planet constantly. It is a form to embody an intention with integrity. When we balance the Seven Tonalities, we tune into a frequency and vibration in our life, into the grid of consciousness and tune into a positive intention.

I highly recommend people to tune into a positive intention when they practice this active meditation. As we live in constant evolution, in constant movement and influences from within and around us, a regular practice gives us tools to tune and accord those tonalities day-after-day, dream-after-dream, step-by-step on our life's journey.

There are four forms that are taught in this active meditation, which are in tune with the moon cycles and our own inner cycles of development.

More information on this meditation is contained in my book, **La Voie de la resonance: The Pathway of the Resonance.**

Made in the USA
Columbia, SC
20 October 2017